CW00751878

FOR CRETE'S SAKE

FOR CRETE'S SAKE

JERRY H. GILL

EFSTATHIADIS GROUP

Efstathiadis Group S.A.
Agiou Athanasiou Street,
GR - 145 65 Anixi, Attikis

ISBN 960 226 522 1

© Efstathiadis Group S.A. 1995

All rights reserved; no part of this
publication may be reproduced, stored in a
retrieval system or transmitted, in any form
or by any means, electronic, mechanical,
photocopying, recording, or otherwise, without the
prior permission of Efstathiadis Group S.A.

Printed and bound in Greece by Efstathiadis Group S.A.

Table of Contents

Introduction·

The title of this book is, of course, more than a bit misleading. It suggests that the island of Crete stands in need of help from me, and nothing could be further from the truth. The wonderful history, beauty, and people of Crete stand alone and speak for themselves. At the fundamental level this book, like most, is written for its author's sake. It represents my own effort to express, at least partially, the deep connection and gratitude I feel after the many months, spread over twenty years, that I have spent on this island. As a result, Crete lives in me every bit as much as I have lived in Crete. I offer this book of memories and reflections as a token of my appreciation for all that Crete has given me -- for Crete's sake.

I shall not seek to provide a well-rounded introduction to Crete, its history, geography, and culture. There are other books that do these things much better than I ever could. What I present here are my memories of and reflections on my continuing encounter with the land, the people, and the heritage of this glorious island located at the axis of the Mediterranean world. At best these memories and reflections will be fragmentary and idiosyncratic, due to the richness that is Crete and the limited character of my own experience there. Nevertheless, I trust they will provide some enjoyment and insight for those who read the, as well as some sense of satisfaction to the one who is sharing them.

My first encounter with Crete came through reading Nikos Kazantzàkis' <u>Zorba the Greek</u> in the early 1960's. A few years later I read his "autobiography", <u>Report to Greco</u>, which led directly to including a two-day visit to Crete in my initial visit to the Mediterranean world in 1966. I remember being awed by the mountainous terrain, the simplicity of the culture, and the genius of the ancient Minoan architecture. Moreover, the spirit of Crete, as embodied in Kazatzàkis' novels, began to take root in my consciousness, urging me to return. Thus, in the summer of 1972,

I went to Crete to begin writing a manuscript on the philosophical and theological aspects of Kazantzàkis' thought.

I spent over two months on Crete and, although the manuscript I produced never became a book, I did fall deeply in love with the island. As a result, I have returned many times and have managed to introduce a large number of my friends and students including my wife to my "second home," as well. At present we are extremely privileged to be able to spend five or six months a year living on Crete as co-directors of the semester abroad program sponsored by the college at which we teach. Over the years we have explored a great many places on the island and made a large number of friends, most of which will find their way into the following remembrances and explorations.

Before actually commencing this personal odyssey, however, a brief introduction of our subject is in order. Crete is located in the middle of the Mediterranean Sea, halfway between Greece and North Africa. It is about 150 miles long and between 40 to 20 miles wide, depending on the coastline. The island comprises three extremely rugged mountain ranges high enough to have snow on them well into the summer. There are two or three major plateaus, virtually no lakes or rivers, and endless beaches. The climate is mild though wet in winter, absolutely wonderful in spring and fall, and extremely warm and dry in summer. Fortunately, during the summer months there is a steady, northerly wind which serves to keep the heat within a comfortable range.

The coastline and mountains of Crete are dotted with literally thousands of tiny villages, connected by a complex and rather unpredictable system of small roads and crowded buses. In addition, there are a few large towns and one major city, Iràklion. Most of these population centers are unfortunately inundated with tourists, together with the technological pollution that accompanies "civilized" living. Fortunately, there are many small towns and villages where a reasonable amount of traditional Cretan culture still thrives. Unlike many other Greek islands, Crete provides ample opportunity to get away from tourism altogether. The remote beaches and mountain roads offer solitude, while the small villages invite interaction with the friendly and proud people of Crete.

The history of Crete began with the Minoan civilization which thrived as an independent culture, while maintaining active trade with the entire Mediterranean world, from at least 2500 B.C. to about 1500 B.C. when it was destroyed by a combination of catastrophic earthquakes and the rising warrior culture of mainland Mycenae. In classical times it was part of the Greek and Roman empires, while throughout the middle ages it participated in the ups and downs of various versions of Christianity. For about 400 years, until 1898, Crete was under the domination of Islamic Turkey, yet managed to maintain most of its traditional culture and Orthodox faith. In the 20th century Crete continued to be ravaged by wars and political upheaval, being occupied by both Nazi and Italian forces in the early 1940's. Since the second World War Crete, along with mainland Greece, has been struggling to find its way into the modern world without losing its traditional identity.

Because of this long and chaotic history, the people of Crete are both proud and a bit suspicious; proud of their noble heritage and their survival capacities, yet suspicious of foreigners who might exploit them. At the same time, however, since tourism is and undoubtedly will remain their primary industry, the people of Crete find it necessary to place themselves in positions which beg for such exploitation. This, along with the fallout from the technological revolution which has swamped the island in the past twenty years, creates a great deal of personal and cultural schizophrenia among contemporary Cretans.

Today many young people, raised within the rich, yet admittedly confining traditional village culture, find themselves at school or work in the midst of rapidly paced capitalist economy, which is at once both liberating and alienating. While the older people of Crete admire modern democratic culture, remembering with deep gratitude its defeat of fascism, the younger folk resent continuously being on the short end of the stick in relation to the economic and military priorities of Western Europe and America. Nevertheless, the vast majority of Crete's citizens are quite capable of distinguishing between the government and the people of a given nation.

This, then, is the island I came to in June of 1972, and with which I have been fortunate to form an enriching relationship over the past twenty years. For those readers who have not as yet ventured to the shores of this magical island, I trust that the following memories and reflections will serve as an invitation, indeed, as an enticement, for you to do so. For those who already have been introduced to the majesty and mystery that is Crete, I hope that the ensuing pages will stimulate and blend in with your own memories and reflections -- and motivate you to undertake the pleasurable task of acquiring even more.

The twelve hour, overnight ferry ride from Pirteus to Crete was an event in itself. The ship was full of peasant-folk, loaded down with packages and children, along with several hundred late-blooming, nomadic "flower children" a few regular-tourist-types, and some Athenians on vacation. After watching my first Mediterranean sunset, I sat around the lounge area watching an ancient Cretan "Palikàri" entertain the other Greek passengers with his stories. A Palikàri is a mountain warrior renowned for his strength and courage. This one was dressed in the traditional garb: black knee high boots, baggy riding pants, a black shirt, wooden shepherd's staff, and a black lace headband. I was especially taken by his snow white beard and twinkling eyes. At dawn from the deck the mountainous silhouette of Crete came into view, looming high above the sea. Little did I realize that it was a sight I would witness and look forward to many times in the years to come. An old woman standing nearby whispered out of awe and respect: "Kriti."

After spending a day or two in Irtklion getting acclimated, paying my respects to the partially restored Minoan palace at Knossos and Kazantzàkis' grave, I entered the new, but tiny office of a travel agency called "Cretan Holidays" in search of advise about an out-of-the-way, seaside site where I might begin my work on Kazantzàkis' thought. Once again, I had no way of knowing that this would be the beginning of a long and deep friendship with the young couple just starting their business. Kostas and Roswitha were very friendly and helpful suggesting that I rent a car and drive East along the Northern coast of the island until I found a suitable village.

Kostas is the youngest man in a Cretan family famous for leading the underground forces against the Nazi occupation. His father was killed and his mother and 14 year old brother taken prisoner. Kostas was born in prison. His brother escaped, found his uncle in the mountains, and together they joined up with British forces in Egypt. Kostas' brother, Zacharias became the youngest airplane pilot in the Second World War. After the war he assumed the role as head of his father's family, vowing never to have a family of his own. While Zacharias worked as a bus driver, Kostas spent several years in the Greek merchant marines travelling all over the world. His wife Roswitha came from Austria, a few years before, fell in love with Kostas' Zorba-like character, and decided to make her life in Crete. She passed the two year course required to be an official Cretan guide, became fluent in Greek, and together they were opening up their own travel agency.

Before allowing me to set off on the journey across Crete, Kostas and Roswitha insisted on taking me out to dinner. During the conversation over a large bottle of Retsina, Kostas sought to give me some insight into Cretan culture. He challenged me to leave my wallet in the street overnight and promised that it would either still be there in the morning, or it would be waiting at the police station. "On the other hand," he said, "if you mess around with my sister, I shall kill you and no one will even investigate the matter." Although things have changed a good deal since then, mostly due to the influx of tourist crime, the juxtaposition of these two scenarios clearly illustrates two dominate characteristics of Cretan culture, honesty and loyalty. Through the ensuing year I have come to experience both of these qualities many times over, especially in friendship and business with Kostas and Roswitha.

The next morning I drove along the coast, poking around a bit in several seaside communities. Somehow none of them seemed to be quite right. Around noon, driving on a new stretch of highway high above the sea, with a view reminiscent of the northern California coastline, I came to a town named Sfa-

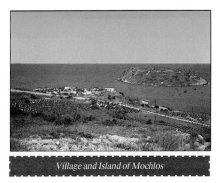
Village and Island of Mochlos

ka. About to enter the town, I noticed a small sign pointing down a winding dirt road headed toward the sea. "Mochlos" was all it said. For some reason I took this road, a decision that turned out to be one of the most important in my life. A mile or two down the road, around a sharp bend, there was a beautiful, fertile seaside plateau surrounding a tiny village, punctuated by a small, round island. It looked warmly and strangely inviting.

I parked the car on the edge of the road and approached an elderly woman, the only person available. In practiced but broken Greek I asked about a room. She smiled, hustled off, and returned with a middle-aged woman, whose name turned out to be Krysùlla. She wrote down a number that stood for the monthly rent. Having been told that in Mediterranean countries bargaining is expected, I wrote down a slightly smaller figure. Krysùlla huffed and walked back down the dirt road to her home. Embarrassed, I followed and agreed to her terms. She introduced me to her husband, Yorgos, and showed me a lovely two room apartment with a toilet and primitive shower just off the grape arbored patio.

Yorgos and Krysùlla in Mochlos

Yorgos had lost an arm working in a nearby gypsum mine, but he was extremely direct and friendly. We made arrangements for me to return by bus the next day to Tourloti, the village just beyond Sfakia where he and Krysulla lived in the winter months. It turned out that not only were they moving out of the two rooms I was taking, into the back of the house, but I was literally the first person who had ever rented a room in Mochlos. It also turned out that these two people, together with their son Nikos, became my oldest and dearest friends in this village. They are still there, having transformed their house into a small hotel, and I am still renting rooms from them. We still haggle over the rent, but now I am trying to pay and they are refusing to take my money.

No one in Mochlos except for Nikos, spoke English, and he was away on "business." When I wrote down Yorgos' full name in Greek, using the writing skills from theological school, he was astounded. He did not understand how someone who could hardly speak Greek at all could in fact read and write it. It was there and then that my anger at not having been taught New Testament and ancient Greek with modern pronunciation was born. Although there are some vocabulary and grammatical differences, as well as half a dozen or so differences in vowel pronunciation, this is no justification for teaching Greek as if it were like Latin, a dead language. It took quite some time to overcome my "classical" heritage, although my major difficulties with Greek derive from having initially learned it from books rather than from conversation.

The next day after meeting the bus in Tourloti, Nikos drove me in his pickup down to Mochlos. He spoke good, simple English and was extremely friendly. He was about twenty years old, played the guitar and sang Mikis Theodorakis songs, music which had been banned by the military Junta running Greece at that time. Krysulla and Yorgos ran a potato-chip "factory" in their home in Tourloti, a one-room operation in which they peeled sliced, cooked, and packaged local potatoes. Nikos delivered the small bags of potato-chips to various stores in nearby towns in his pickup truck. Quite a number of times he took me with him, providing an introduction to many people and places throughout the eastern end of the island. Thus began an on-going love affair with the village of Mochlos.

It did not take long for the basic facts about the village to become clear. There were about 40 people, most of whom spent the winter months in nearby villages and towns along the highway, high

Mochlos resident

up the side of the cliff. Mochlos also serves as a kind of summer "resort" for village folk up and down the northeast coast of Crete. Electricity did not come to the village until 1982, so all the lighting was by kerosene lamps and lanterns. There were two taverans by the sea, one of which had a generator and provided minimal refrigeration. The village was laid out around a small natural harbor, the thirty or so one-story homes all facing the water where the small fishing boats were anchored. The two streets intersected each other right outside the house I was living in, the one running parallel to the shore for about a half kilometer and the other running about an equal distance from the shore on up the hill.

The chief occupation, unsurprisingly, was fishing, and early every morning nearly the whole village gathered around the cement dock to consider the day's catch. The other gathering place was the main -- and only -- intersection, where the women came to fill their water buckets during the daily hour that running water was available. In addition, some of the houses, like mine, had large, fresh water cistern beneath them. Some of the men were farmers, raising wheat, grapes, and as elsewhere in Greece, nearly every family owned a large number of the thousands of olive trees which dotted the entire landscape. Very few of these folks were economically "successful" by Western standards. However, as I was about to discover, they lived full, productive, and pleasant lives raising families, going to school, and finding sufficient work. The most remarkable thing about them was their ability to harmonize the fulfilling of their basic needs with an ever ready capacity to enjoy nature, the present, and one another.

Mochlos is significantly isolated from the other villages and towns nearby, lying as it does on the coast at the end of a winding, five mile road connecting it with the highway several thousand feet up the mountain. Hiking up takes about two hours. Between the mountains which form the southward landscape and the coast a number of foothills roll down to the sea. The sun rises out to the water in the East, on the right as one stands facing the sea, traverses the incredibly blue sky overhead, and sets behind the low coastline near the town of Agios Nikolaos in the West, on the left. Directly in front of the village, about 200 yards out, sits Mochlos islet. It is around a quarter of a mile in diameter, two hundred feet high, and quite rocky. Before a relatively modern earthquake, it was attached to the coast of Crete by a spit of land and on a calm day one can see the remains of the stone road leading out there. In recent years a very significant Minoan excavation has been conducted there during the summer months, filling the village with American and Greek archaeologists.

The first day I met a woman in her 80's, Irini, who live down the road a bit in a one-room house with her husband, Manoli. As I walked by she was sweeping her dirt floor, all bent over. She pointed to her goat and chickens behind the wire fence, and asked it I would like some milk (gàla) or an egg (avgà). It was arranged, in minimal Greek, that she would deliver milk and eggs to the house every morning for my breakfast. It was not made clear at the time that she milked the goat and collected the eggs at 5 a.m. Irini assumed that

Mochlos Woman Irene

was when she would make her delivery. I found out about it the next morning when Irini began pounding on the shutters and yelling "Gàla" and "Avgà." Fortunately I was able to stall the regular delivery off until 6 a.m. thereafter. This illustrates the point that the day begins very early in Mochlos; folks rise with the sun.

I soon settled down to a routine of writing in the room during the mornings, swimming and reading, or hiking in the sun in the afternoon. Evenings were spent dining at one of the two tavernas and spending several hours listening village conversation over a number of bottles of wine. The food and wine, though quite repetitious, were always excellent. The fare was one dish per evening, usually salad, stuffed vegetables, fish or lamb, followed by cheese and fruit. The wine was local, bottled Retsina, or raki, the Cretan version of "white lightnin." The cost for the meals, like that for the rooms, was ridiculously low. The villagers followed the Mediterranean custom of staying up late at night, talking, eating, and drinking, rising early in the morning for work, and then resting for three hours or so after the noontime meal, thus avoiding the hot afternoon sun. Nearly everything closed down between 2 and 5 p.m.

I became, by reason of circumstance, something of a celebrity in the village, partly because I was the only outsider, partly because I was an American, but mostly because I was writing a manuscript about Nikos Kazantzàkis. The people asked many questions about my life and about America, and I had many questions about Crete and their lives in return. They all knew of Kazantzakis' writings, most had read either Zorba The Greek or Freedom or Death, and many had personal stories to tell which connected up with or parallel his in some way. The latter book depicts Cretan rebellion against Turkish oppression. In addition to being a national hero because of the quality and fame of his writing, Kazantzakis symbolized the courage and independence that all Cretans experience simply by growing up there.

Moreover, Kazantzakis was the first successful author to be able to publish his works in demotic rather than "purified" Greek. This meant that his novels, which are chockful of idiomatic and dialectic expressions from the speech of peasants and fisherman, could be fully understood and appreciated by these very people. Although the Bishop of Athens would not allow Kazantzakis to be buried on mainland Greece when he died in 1954, the Bishop of Crete welcomed the "favorite son" to a burial spot of honor in Iraklion, and declared an official holiday. Five thousand people turned out for the funeral and hundreds of school children carried copies of his various books in different translations in the processional. Small wonder the people of Mochlos were pleased to have me and my writing project as their guests. At first nearly all of my participation in the evening conversations was filtered through Nikos' translations, but as the weeks went by Greek began to come more accessible. Not ever having been a late-night person, I was usually in bed well before the taverna lanterns were extinguished. The morning writing went well and afternoon explorations revealed many wonders. The extremely clear water, together with the rocky cliffs of the shoreline, provided ample challenge and beauty for eager but tame snorkeling adventures. Two or three times a week rugged, mountain hillsides yielded to my ambitious hiking and scrambling, the reward being numerous breathtaking views, coupled with very tired but sturdier muscles.

Every now and then Nikos would take me with him in his delivery truck. After dropping off the potato chips we would shop for necessities and spend a couple of hours sipping near-eastern coffee, conversing. Agios, Nikolaos, Sitia, and Ierapetra became familiar realities, and I learned a lot about the sense of loss and paralysis experienced by many contemporary Cretans. Nikos felt he had no future in rural Crete, that he must move to Iraklion,

Athens, or beyond in order to survive the transition from a declining, traditional culture to a modern, technological one. One day, seated in a remote outdoor taverna by the sea he said: "You know, people always speak about the greatness and glory of Greece. But I look around and I don't see such things; I see the very opposite."

In addition to Nikos and his parents, Mochlos blessed me with two other special friends, Philipas and Katina. A sweet and lively elderly couple, they ran the smaller of the two tavernas in town and had been married for fifty years. They also owned a tiny, but lovely two-room retirement cottage on the hillside above the village, complete with an absolutely spectacular view of the mountainous coastline and some outlying island. Katina had a face like a round warm, smiling olive, with quick, fun loving eyes and a cackling laugh. She hustled around making sure everything got done and everyone was satisfied. Philipas was tall and angular, with a large nose and a shock of white hair. He was an exceptional pantomime artist and story-teller. We spent many long evenings together acting out our conversation as we went along. Our initial encounter was particularly memorable.

Philipas and Katina

The first day in Mochlos Philipas was seated outside of his taverna. In simple, but practiced Greek I asked: "Do you have bread?" He neither moved nor spoke. Once again: "Do you have bread?" Once more, no response. After asking yet again, I noticed that all along Philipas had been answering my question with a slight upward movement of his head and his eyes. It turns out that this is the common Greek way of saying "No." Then, rising from his chair and moving through the door into the taverna, he extended his arm and began waving his hand back and forth between us, with his fingers pointing downward. Since the movement looked a lot like how we Americans shoo someone away, I was completely confused about what to do. It finally became clear that the thrust of his hand movement was <u>toward</u> himself rather than <u>away</u>, so I followed him inside. He did have some twice or "sundried" bread, called "paxamàdi," which he offered me as a gift. Not knowing the Greek word for this special, extremely hard bread, I with my limited vocabulary thanked him for the "pètra psomi," which literally means "rock bread." Philipas' enjoyment of this little joke became the initial foothold for our ensuing friendship.

One other significant "personage" in Mochlos was the high cliff a mile or so directly to the east of the village. Not only did it dominate the landscape, rising straight up over a thousand feet out of the sea, but its "personality" went through a fascinating number of changes throughout the day. In the early morning, with the sun rising behind it, the cliff appeared as a solid black silhouette, like a gigantic cardboard theater background. At mid-day the sun shown directly down on the cliff so as to accentuate its jagged lines, crevasses, and caves. In the afternoon the cliff turned a variety of shades of purple and grey, while at sunset it took on a deep, misty blue color. It was entirely possible to spend a whole day simply watching the cliff put on its show. Rarely an evening went by that we did not devote an hour or two gazing at the transforming cliffside. It sure beat watching television.

Leaving Mochlos and all my new friends after six weeks of such peaceful, enriching existence was extremely difficult. Hiking up to Sfàka, my mind full of smiling faces and tearful eyes, I knew that this tiny village had become an extremely important reality in my life. Although I had no specific plans for a return visit, it was certain that one would take place. As Pascal said: "The heart has reasons which reason knows not of."

I returned to Mochlos three years later with a group of 15 students. I had arranged a six week summer session in Greece with the college where I was teaching and we were spending four week in Mochlos. The students were enrolled in two courses, one on "Greek Culture" and the other on "The Thought of Nikos Kazantzàkis." The former course included an introduction to modern Greek, as well to Minoan, classical, and contemporary Greek civilization. Krysùla and Yorgos had become managers of one of the tavernas, and they had transformed their home into a small hotel with six rooms. By enlisting a couple of rooms in neighboring homes, they were able to provide for our board and room needs.

It was, of course, a great joy to be able to share my adopted village home with my students, and vice versa. Mochlos had changed very little, a few new faces and a few absent ones. The students had some difficulty at first adjusting to the incredibly slow pace and the daily routine of having "nothing to do." Soon, however, the magic of the weather, the natural beauty, and the charm of the people began to work on them. When it came time to leave, it was difficult to do so. The village folk had taught us some Cretan songs and dances, and the students in turn had played soccer with the children and performed a simple play in Greek for the whole village. As they say, "There wasn't a dry eye in the place" as we prepared to hike up to the highway for the last time. Two of the male students actually managed to repeat the summer session again the following year, and several others, from both this group and succeeding groups, have managed return visits to Mochlos over the years. The place has a way of getting inside of you.

The most significant story of this initial return trip involves a student named Theresa. At first meeting it was clear that Theresa was a unique individual. As an art major she brought a special interest and knowledge to her encounter with Greece, and even before the summer session had begun she was learning Greek

in a serious way from an exchange student on campus. Throughout our six weeks in Greece she absorbed the culture and the language like a sponge, being especially taken with the philosophy of life embodied in Kazantzakis' major characters. It was as if Theresa had been born in the wrong country and had finally found her rightful place. In fact, in a letter a couple of years later, she thanked me for having brought her "to my true home, Mochlos."

The primary focus of Theresa's somewhat "romantic" interaction

Teresa

with Mochlos was her quite serious romance with a local fisherman named Mihàlis. While she was participating fully in the academic program and spending a great deal of time talking to and swimming with the children of the village, she was, somewhat surreptitiously, falling head-over-heels in love. The full reality of this development did not surface until our last day in Mochlos, when Theresa, whose name was now pronounced "Terèsa," announced that after spending the next school year in Florence studying art, she would be returning to Mochlos and Mihàlis permanently. And she did! Indeed, after completing her college degree the year after that, she returned again to Mochlos, married Mihàlis, and began her family. Although it makes a wonderful story with which to entice students to visit Greece, it is not one calculated to set their parents' hearts and minds to rest.

Terèsa spent her early years in Mochlos working on their fishing boat with Mihàlis. Later on she cultivated a rather elaborate garden and kept a goat. Along the way she found time to continue with her art work, at least minimally with watercolors and taking up quiltmaking. Terèsa's dark skin and hair coloring, her incredible facility for languages, and her natural strength and flexibility of character, enabled her to adapt to and adopt the culture of Crete with amazing speed and thoroughness. After a few years, even native Cretans were unable to discern that she was not Greek. In addition to all this, Terèsa managed to collect and read a great number of books on a wide variety of topics. She became my main contact person in arranging for future student groups and I became her main outside source of books and art supplies.

In this way my heart became even more tightly bound up with this tiny Cretan village. Not only had Mochlos been my gift, as it were, to Terèsa, but she had become my gift to Mochlos, as well. The villagers were and remain extremely proud of her, in addition to simply enjoying her as a member of their community. Of course Mihàlis, who is every bit as unique as Terèsa, was the most pleased of all, and we, too, became good friends. After having travelled around the world as a merchant mariner, he had decided that Mochlos was, after all, the best place to live. It was impossible not to think that both he and Terèsa had made the right decision.

There was one other incident that took place during this first summer session in Mochlos which reveals yet another distinctive facet of village life on Crete. A few days after arriving I paid half of the money for our board and room for the month to Yorgos. Even though the cost of living is minimal in Greece, food and rooms for 16 people for 30 days came to a sizable sum, especially by village standards. Two days later rumor had it that someone had stolen the money. As politely as possible, I asked Yorgos what had happened. He described how he had hung his jacket, with the money in it, in the back room of the taverna where he and Krysulla slept. Someone had taken the money while they were working in the kitchen.

The next obvious move, it would seem, would be to call the police from Sfàka and find out who had stolen the money. But Yorgos indicated that he knew who the thief was, and that he was right there in the taveran this very moment. When I asked what he was going to do about the situation, he replied that after a few months or years, when the time was ripe, he would find a way to steal the money back. After all, he and the man who took the money had grown up together in these villages all these years without having recourse to police and such, so why change things now. In any case, traditional village justice is at once much more direct and patient, he said. I have often pondered the pros and cons of Yorgos' way of dealing with this incident, and several times have made up my mind to ask him about its outcome. But I always conclude that it is not really an outsider's business.

In the summer of 1981 I returned to Crete, this time without students, spending the entire month of July in Mochlos. Although my daily routine remained pretty much the same as that of my initial visit, the village itself was now quite different. Nikos had been spending his winter working in a restaurant-bar in Germany, where he made a great number of friends. He began inviting these folks to Mochlos and slowly they, along with other northern European visitors transformed the village into something of a tourist attraction. In addition to the rooms provided by Nikos' parents, there were now three other hotels and two new tavernas. Over a period of five or six months, between April and September, Mochlos now served as host to several hundred visitors a year. It has become, quite surprisingly, a rather cosmopolitan center.

It was, to be sure, an extremely off-beat type of "tourist" that would seek out this remote and basically simple village for a two to four week vacation. Most of the people I came to know were educators, students, writers and artists of a distinctly grass-roots sort. After all, the main attractions, aside from the lively evening conversations in the tavernas, were still only natural beauty, peace and quiet, and the view of the ever-changing cliffside. During the month in Mochlos that summer, I met several students from Switzerland, high school teachers from Germany, a writer from Denmark, and several French folk, who seemed to be perpetual vacationers. In addition, there were now several foreign women who, following Terèsa's lead, had settled down with men from the village and were now raising families there. They were from Germany, France, Canada, and Switzerland, and they frequently worked in the local taverans and hotels.

Terèsa's children, Margarita and Yorgos, were still quite young, but they seemed to enjoy the life of the village very much. One of the amazing and beautiful things about Mochlos, and perhaps all such places, is that the children are free and safe playing in and around the houses, hotels, and tavernas, even by the seaside. Not only are the parents confident that some adult in the community knows where each and every child is at any given moment, but the children look out after each other, as well. Terèsa had become close friends with several of the new mothers in the village, one of whom was now married to Mihàlis' brother Manoli. She also was friends with many of the European "regulars" and especially enjoyed the visits her two younger sisters made to Mochlos from America.

There were a number of new Greek people living in the village now, as well. I became friends with Fotini and Spiro, daughter and son of the couple who operated one of the new tavernas. They had just recently graduated from high school in nearby Sitia and worked as waiters in their parent's place, bringing a great deal of life and warmth with their friendly and efficient manner. Their's is a friendship which I very much enjoy, even to this day. During the afternoons when I was not out hiking or swimming, I often played soccer and basketball with the three young boys who were now spending their summers in Mochlos, Nikos, Nektàrios, and yet another Nikos. It has been a real pleasure to watch them grow over the years and now to know them as young adults, though I must confess that the Greek custom of naming the firstborn son after the father's father sometimes gets as annoying as it is confusing. I would guess that about half of the men in Greece share six basic names: Yorgos, Manoli, Yànis, Mihàlis, Vangèli, and, of course, Nikos. In a place the size of Mochlos this gets to be a problem.

Along with my usual writing projects, sculpting in stone had recently become one of my avocations. In the mountain directly above and behind Mochlos was a gypsum mine where they simply discarded whatever quartz and alabaster chunks which got in the way. These stones, somewhat crystaly and soft in consistency and black and white in color, are relatively easy to work with a file and rough sandpaper. I spent my evenings in an out-of-the-way corner of the tavernas working on my stones and listening to the conversations. It was an excellent way to sharpen my ear for the Greek language. One evening young Nektàrios, watching me work on an abstract form, asked: "Ti eènay?" (What is it?) I tried to explain that it was meant to be a dolphin, even though it did not look much like one. He smiled knowingly and exclaimed: "Delfini pnèvma!" (Dolphin spirit). I shared this story with Kostas, my travel agent friend in Iraklion, when I gave the sculpture to him and Roswitha.

My main hiking adventure that summer was to climb up and over the giant and multi-colored cliff to a deserted village on the other side. To be sure, I went up the side of the cliff, not up its formidable face. Even this proved to be an extremely difficult task, one which would involve several hours of hiking to and from the cliff. Along the way I investigated the ruins of a small Venetian fortress, dating form the 14th century, from the tower of which one would have had a commanding view of at least twenty miles of coastline. The thick, sage underbrush above the olive groves was as rough on my short-panted legs as the sun was on my hatless bald head. However, the latter was more accustomed to such treatment than were the former.

The view from the top of the cliff was truly spectacular, an excellent spot to pause for lunch before exploring the deserted village below. There was nothing spooky about the quiet, peopleless paths and houses perched on the edge of the cliff. It was easy to imagine what life was like there in years gone by. They say that in late fall a number of farmers gather in this village to facilitate the harvesting of nearby olive trees. Then for a few weeks the place comes alive once more with the songs and laughter so characteristic of Cretan village life. The peaceful presence of this unusual spot remained with me throughout the hike back to

Mochlos.

The other major adventure of this particular stay in Mochlos was not nearly so peaceful or serious. One day Mihàlis asked if I would like to go fishing with him and his brother Manoli the next morning. Delighted by the prospect of working side by side with these village fishermen on their small boat on the open sea, I eagerly awaited them on the dock before dawn. Leaving the protected bay of Mochlos behind, we headed for the base of the great cliff, along which we would lay the mile-long fishnet and wait for the fish to move at sunrise. All went heroically until we began to drop the net. The small boat was positioned sideways in relation to the cliff and moved along slowly parallel to it. This meant that it was rocked by the waves both as they came in toward to cliff and as they recoiled off it. This constant and rather rapid motion immediately made me extremely seasick, rendering me completely useless to the voyage. I lay on the deck, head hanging over the edge, and comforted myself with the thought that because this episode would be over as soon as we returned to the village, it was not as bad as being sick with, say, the flu.

We pulled into a quiet inlet to wait for the fish to move and my innards calmed down a bit. While Mihàlis and Manoli were taking the net in, however, it was to quote Yogi Berra, "deja vu all over again." On the way home all my stomach could think of was filling itself with bread and coca-cola. Throughout the ordeal the two brothers were extremely embarrassed and sorry for me, constantly checking to see if I was alright. So much for my bold, Homeric sea venture. The worst part, however, is that this ordeal had to be repeated three times before the lesson was learned; the lesson presumably being that landlubbing penpushers should not try to be sailors as well. The happy part of this adventure is that the brothers and I became closer friends and one taveran sold more than its share of bread and coca-cola for breakfast.

Two years later in 1983, I had the wonderful experience of being able to share Crete and Mochlos with my wife, Mari Sorri. We had been married the year before and had agreed to divide our summer vacation between her native home in rural Finland and my adopted home in Crete. As a wedding present, Kostas and Roswitha gave us two weeks in one of their resorts on the beach in Rèthymnon at the western end of the island. Although we greatly enjoyed those "five star" days, especially the visits with Kostas, Roswitha, and their children, we both looked forward to getting on to the simple ambiance of life in a small village. We stayed a month, and in full accord with my expectations, the people of Mochlos received Mari as one of them and she, in turn, immediately fell in love with all of them.

In the two years since my last visit, Mochlos had continued to grow and change. Full electric power and telephone connections had been installed, and one of the tavernas now had a television on which the village children watched reruns of "Zorro." There were two new small hotels as well, and more Greek people from both Crete and Athens were spending their vacations in Mochlos. In fact, there was now a small store sporting the English sign: "Supermarket." A few miles down the coast some German entrepreneurs had built a large, snazzy resort hotel, with pools, tennis courts, and its own newly built beach. Once a day the small hotel bus brought some tourists to Mochlos to sample authentic village life. So it was that on any given day there were upwards of one hundred people in Mochlos. On the weekends, especially in the evenings, there were even more.

Another new facet of village life was the presence of two teams of archaeologists. Both Minoan excavations were jointly sponsored by American universities and the Greek government, one located on the nearby island of Psira and the other on the tiny islet of Mochlos itself. Together there were about fifty people involved in the digs, but only about half of them stayed in the village. The others were local Greek workmen who lived in other nearby towns. In addition to providing a new dimension to the evening taverna conversations, the archaeologists, most of whom were students, brought both extra money and the sense of pride to the villagers. Cretans are rightfully proud of their Minoan heritage, the presence of which is always more evident to them than that of classical Greece.

In recent years Minoan excavations at the eastern end of Crete have received an increasing amount of public attention, altering significantly the historical and cultural interpretations of ancient Mediterranean civilization. In fact, Mochlos and Sitia were given two-page coverage in the "Travel" section of the Sunday edition of the New York Times on June 15, 1991. For several years one of these excavations has provided Terèsa with an excellent job as an archaeological artist. All of the artifacts are brought back to Mochlos for identification and cataloguing, and she is responsible for providing graphic renderings of the more significant pieces. Her husband, Mihàlis, uses his boat to ferry the workers to and from the island. Needless to say, we eagerly avail ourselves of every opportunity to visit these excavations and to gather whatever information we can about Minoan culture and history from Terèsa and her co-workers.

The influx of all these "outsiders" stimulated us to spend more time with folks who lived a bit off the beaten path of the village. My long-time friends Philipas and Katina had retired permanently to their little cottage on the hillside above Mochlos, near the new, but still primitive road down to the sea. We spent several evenings with them, watching the sunset, sharing a meal, and visiting with the family who lived across the road. My clearest memories are of giving one of the family's children a "horsy-back" ride on my foot while sitting cross-legged in a chair. I can still hear his uncontrollable laughter and pleas for me to continue whenever I paused to rest my leg: "Pàli, pàli" (Again, again). Also the image of the huge sunflowers surrounding Philipas' home frequently presents itself.

Mari and I made new friends that year, an elderly basketmaker named Yànis and his wife Dèspina. They spend their summers in a one room cottage, complete with grape arbor and dirt patio, just above the main road about a kilometer before you arrive in Mochlos. Yànis builds various sized baskets out of bamboo and grapevines, a complex art requiring a knowledge of moon cycles for the timely cutting of the bamboo. These baskets are extremely strong, as is proved by the fact that the one which we bought that summer we are still using to carry firewood for a woodstove at home.

Over the years since then we always introduce our students and friends to Yànis, and he provides a brief demonstration of his art, Dèspina, whom Yànis calls "Kùkla," which means "Baby", provides large amounts of stuffed vine leaves, tomatoes, and zucchini flowers, along with ample raki. Very few drink much, if any, raki, but nearly everyone buys several baskets. Yànis and Dèspina know no English and often rattle on so fast in Greek as to leave us all behind. But it doesn't matter much, since there are important levels and qualities of human communication

Yànis the basket maker

established by smiles, tones, postures, and looks. It is always clear that everyone, including Yànis and Dèspina, enjoy these times together very much.

As was mentioned above, Mari and I began bringing groups of students and friends to Greece for month-long tours. On these occasions we always arrange to stay two weeks in Mochlos, and nearly everyone agrees that this is the best part of the trip, one that includes visits to the exotic island of Santorini, Delphi, and Athens. There is, of course, always a certain amount of culture shock when people from a highly technological culture, who are used to the amenities and affluence it provides, stay in a place where the water is in short supply, the food is simple and repetitive, and you burn your own toilet paper rather than flushing it down the drain. In spite of this, these who have made these trips continue to rave about the, and some even make return visits to Mochlos on their own.

On one such summer excursion we were informed that up in the hills a large sheep shearing party was going to take place, an event which should not be missed. Since we are in the practice of taking our groups on longish hikes, we jumped at this opportunity. We arranged for two pickup trucks to take us all to the highway, and then we started our trek up the long zig-zag farming road cut into the side of the steep mountain rising up from the sea behind Mochlos. Everyone assured us that once the large plateau at the top of the mountain was reached, locating the sheep shearing site would be a simple matter. After stopping for rest and nourishment at the edge of the plateau, we hiked on through a mountain pass to an other farm road as a shepherd along the way had indicated that it was only a little way further on down the road.

Four hours after the journey began it finally came to an end at a small farm where a large corral had been set up. There were a half a dozen men there busily shearing what looked like a thousand sheep. They took turns wrestling the sheep to the ground and cutting off the wool with large hand-scissors. The men seemed pleased to have an audience, throwing themselves into their work with renewed enthusiasm. The whole event was not the sort of spectacle one gets to witness very often, especially if one is a " city-slicker," as most of us were. The students took many pictures of and with the sheepshearders, who were obviously proud to be viewed with such importance.

While we were resting and eating, the reality of the four hour return trip began to dawn. There was, of course, no option but to retrace our steps through the pass, across the plateau, and down the mountain zig-zag. The beauty of the coastal landscape which spread before us the whole way home more than compensated for the fatigue involved. Along the way everyone was grateful that this part of the journey was all down hill. The bad news was that the next morning everyone had extremely sore feet and severe pain in previously unknown muscles, especially in the front of their thighs. If you are not used to it, hiking down hill can be every bit as consequential as its uphill counterpart. All in all it was quite an adventure. As one student put it: "Its all part of the Cretan experience."

As was mentioned a couple of times before, some of our students have enjoyed Mochlos so much they have found their way back to it sooner or later. One such person is Tim from Albany, New York. On his first visit, Tim proved to be one of the most eager and exploratory students one can imagine. In addition to participating fully in every aspect of the planned program, which was always packed full, he continuously sought out ways to know Crete and himself better. Frequently this resulted in our having to wait and/or search for him, and occasionally it meant that he found himself in trouble, but all such inconveniences were well worth his enthusiasm and personal growth. Tim studies both philosophy and art, and whether he was pursuing an important aspect of Kazantzàkis' thought or a remote perspective for a landscape drawing, his energy and unique insights were always evident and valuable.

At the conclusion of his second summer visit, Tim decided to stay in Crete for the entire year. Having just graduated from college, he had no immediate plans or obligations, so why not? With some financial backing from Bill, another "two-timer" who will be introduced more formally shortly, and the promise of some winter work in one of Kostas and Roswitha's hotels, Tim felt sufficiently secure to take on this adventure. For the remainder of the summer he worked with the archaeologists, in the Fall he did odd-jobs, including babysitting for Terèsa, and in the spring he travelled throughout mainland Greece. In addition to greatly improving his Greek, Tim grew tremendously as an artist and as a person by virtue of this experience.

A year after his return to the United States, Tim began work on an interdisciplinary master's degree and was able to arrange to do two courses independently while visiting Crete yet a third time. By then Mari and I had begun directing a full semester in Greece program in Sitia every Fall. Tim was able to co-ordinate his studies and living arrangements in such a way as to participate with the undergraduates to some degree. It was very gratifying to see him function on Crete on his own, and he also set a challenging example for the less-adventuresome students in our new program. At this writing, Tim is hoping to begin studying for an interdisciplinary doctoral degree, with concrete plans of returning again to Crete before very long.

Another intrepid explorer, one who was 79 years young when he first accompanied us to Crete, is Bill. When we first met, Bill was a widower who had already been to Europe 17 times. He liked the idea of travelling at the grass-roots level (what some people would call "third class") and he very much enjoyed the company of college students. In addition to being fluent in Italian, Bill also knew some Greek, having already been to Greece on his own some years before. We travelled almost always by local transportation, carrying a backpack and living in very simple accommodations. Bill adjusted to this style very well. Moreover,

Students in Mochlos with Bill (with white hair)

he participated in nearly every activity, except for the long hikes, right along with the students, including optional sessions on the Minoans, the Greek language, and Kazantzakis. Little wonder we were delighted to have Bill sign up for a second trip with us two years later.

It was Bill who helped finance Tim's year-long stay on Crete, and he frequently made everyone in the group recipients of small gifts, such as bottles of wine, tourist T-shirts, or ice-cream cones. On his second trip with us, Bill became especially close friends with Tony, a student who was a bit older and more mature than the others. Tony had a listening capacity equal to Bill's story-telling capacity, so they got along very well. Whenever Bill would pause, after having related a fairly surprising turn of events in a given story, Tony would exclaim in astonishment: "Go on!" And, so, Bill would. The two of them added a great deal to the entertainment of the students.

Along with all this, Bill always made many Greek friends, especially in Mochlos. He is genuinely interested in them and they think it is wonderful that he continues to travel and grow on into his 80's. Once we began our Fall Semester in Greece program, situated in Sitia, Bill and Tony not only blessed us with a two-week vacation visit during the second year of the program, but they both provided significant financial support for various enrichment features, such as procuring native Cretan teachers for language and dancing lessons. Whenever either one of these "angels" comes to Crete, we are as pleased to see them as they are to be there. And the people of Mochlos all turn out to greet them when they arrive and to bid them farewell when they leave.

One evening, Mari and I had hiked up to the highway to have dinner at a roadside cafe. After eating we sat on a large boulder and watched the sunset with the shadowy coastal plain of Mochlos spread out below us. Mari said, almost in a whisper, "Wouldn't it be wonderful to be able to live here?" This small remark planted a seed in the south forty of my consciousness. All my life I had moved around following various job opportunities and learning to appreciate whatever benefits the local geography, climate, and culture had to offer. I asked myself: "What about deciding first where you want to live and working to bring the job to you?" A year later we began to lay plans for a regular Semester in Greece program sponsored by the college where we both taught.

We have been co-directing this program for three years now in the city of Sitia, about an hour's drive east from Mochlos. In some ways an account of this adventure could be thought of as the natural sequel to this present chapter. However, during my twenty year affair with the island of Crete I managed to explore other parts and aspects of it, as well as other islands and various well-known sites of classical significance. Since these explorations took place prior to our move to Sitia, it seems appropriate to incorporate them at this juncture, before proceeding to events that bring us closer to the present.

Mochlos Sunrise

Throughout my years of visiting Crete, Mochlos always served as the axis around which other places and journeys revolved. In the same way, Crete has always been the center of my explorations of the wider reaches of Greece itself. Thus, not only is my appreciation of the whole of Greece tethered to Mochlos and Crete, but reciprocally my experience of this adopted home is strongly conditioned by my excursions to other islands and the Greek mainland, as well. This chapter will recount some of the highlights of these travels, moving concentrically from various regions of Crete, through the islands of Santorini and Mykonos, to the famous sites of Olympia, Delphi, and Athens itself. It will conclude with memories of a monastery on the peninsula of Mt. Athos and a climb to the top of Mt. Olympus.

Not far from Mochlos, high up in the mountains, lies the plain or plateau of Lasithi, a picturesque and distinctive spot I enjoy visiting. Its geological situation reminds one of that a Shangri-la, the mythical paradise hidden within the snowy peaks of the Tibetan Himalayas. Unlike its mythical counterpart, however, the Lasithi plateau is usually inundated with snow in the winter. So much so, in fact, that most of the people living in its dozen or so villages spend the winters with relatives who do not live so high on the mountain side. One of the two roads leading up to Lasithi has recently been modernized, but it is still a bit scary to drive, partly because one cannot help being distracted by the absolutely fantastic view of the Cretin mountains and endless coastline. The ever-twisting road carries one through several mountain villages, as yet unmolested by tourist trade.

Winding through the small mountain pass that provides the entrance to the Lasithi plateau, the small road opens up onto an incredibly fertile farming plain. Up until the arrival of electricity, the crops were irrigated with water pumped by over 1,000 windmills, but most of these are now defunct. The twelve tiny, quaint villages are joined by a road that circles the outer rim of the plateau, with the farmland spread out across the central area about three miles across. One of the villages boasts a deep and interesting cavesite where legend has it that Zeus was born. Several guides, complete with donkeys for going up to the cave and candles for going down into it, are available. Nearly all the villages are dotted with roadside cafes and tourist shops which specialize in woven and woolen rugs, blankets, and shawls. The people of Lasithi are extremely friendly, but some have become a tad overbearing when it comes to hawking their goods. It has always been refreshing to visit such mountain locales after having spent so much time on the Cretan coastline.

Over the years of coming and going to and from Crete, one can hardly avoid spending a good deal of time in Iraklion, its capital city. During the past twenty years Iraklion has been transformed by technology and tourism from a somewhat exotic, out of the

Downtown Iraklion

way, semi-Turkish and semi-North African town, into a dirty, noisy, highly congested, and no longer interesting Western city. Although it now offers such enrichments as an international airport and a university, both of these have contributed greatly to the serious over-crowding which may be Iraklion's most obvious characteristic. In spite of these sad facts, however, I have found ways to redeem the time it is necessary to stay in Iraklion. One can still experience peace and traditional Cretan culture by wandering off the beaten path, through the back streets of the older, residential areas. This is an especially nice way to find one's way to the grave of Nikos Kazantzakis, which stands on top of an old Venetian fortress wall, high above the city. These streets are generally too small and twisting for cars, so a walk through the maze they create allows one to encounter small children and older folks, together with the familiar sounds and smells of village life.

Another way to make a stay in Iraklion enjoyable is to include a visit to nearby Knossos, the excavated and partially restored Minoan palace. The intricate and grandiose character of these ruins is truly a marvel to behold, no matter how many times one experiences it. Of course, in the summer it is best to visit Knossós in the early morning or late afternoon when the number of people is far less. Some years back I was able to find a guide in the nearby village of Archanes, who took me to the most recent Minoan excavations in that area, including Amnios Spillo. At this site archaeologists have uncovered a small hill-top temple which was destroyed by earthquake right in the middle of what clearly seems to have been an act of human sacrifice of a young prince. It is the only evidence there is of such a ritual in Minoan sites, thus suggesting that the severity of the earthquake may have prompted the priest to extreme measures. Evidently whatever gods were involved were not pleased with such a sacrifice, for they interrupted it quite abruptly.

For myself, the most satisfying escape from the ravages of the city of Iraklion is the enjoyment of friends. Over these twenty years we have arranged all the transportation aspects of our group excursions through Cretan Holidays. This enables us to visit at least briefly with our friends Kostas and Roswitha, who have become tremendously busy with the great success of their business. In spite of their busy schedule, however, they have frequently entertained our groups either at their home or at their resort hotel 30 kilometers to the East. Cretan hospitality tends to be complete. The host takes care of everything and picks up the check, no questions asked. It means a great deal to us, now that we actually live on Crete half of every year, to be able to extend such hospitality to others, and especially to our Greek friends who have been so kind to us for so many years.

Kostas and Roswitha's children, Zacharias and Despina have now grown up, studying at different European universities and working in their parents' business. It is difficult to exaggerate the loyalty which characterizes this family's friendship. Over the years there have been a number of difficulties, as well as one or two near disasters, that have arisen in our travels to and on Crete. In every case we have been able to count on Kostas and Roswitha to help us out, even bail us out. Surprisingly, this extreme loyalty extends throughout the various folks who work for Cretan Holidays, from office managers and secretaries to tour guides and bus drivers. Doing business with such genuine human beings renders the prospect of visiting Iraklion even more than tolerable.

The very first student group stayed at a small and rather run-down pension in Iraklion named "Mykonos." All subsequent groups have been booked there as well, partly because of its excellent location, just beside the "El Greco" park near the Fountain Square, and partly because of the hospitality of the managers, Manoli and his wife Antiyoni. When we booked their little "hotel" for three or more days, they always provided us with a more than ample continental breakfast, even though they were not officially licensed to do so. Also, they were happy to rearrange the number of beds in their six rooms according to the number of males and females in our group, and according to our limited budget. In addition, the vine-covered patio in the back served very well for our group meetings.

Manoli and Antiyoni originally came from a mountain village about an hour from Iraklion where Manoli still held a regular job as a civil engineer. The village is planning to open a winter resort for skiers. Somehow Manoli manages to drive back and forth to work everyday, still finding time to build them a home in the village. Soon they will move back to the village permanently, when the home is ready and their young son Yorgos is of school age. In the meantime Antiyoni handles nearly all the work at the "M/konos," including doing the laundry and cleaning the rooms, while taking care of Yorgos and baby Maria. In spite of all these responsibilities, these folks remain excellent hosts, while becoming our really good friends. Mari and I have spent a number of evenings in their small living room conversing, listening to Manoli play the lyre, and playing with the children. We shall miss them greatly when they return to their village, but it is clear that their lives will be so much better then.

Another place of special significance on Crete is the Gorge of Samaria. Billed as "the longest, deepest, narrowest gorge in

Samaria Gorge

Europe," it is 18 kilometers long, drops from 4,000 feet to sea level, and at one point is only about four yards across. In Winter the gorge is full of snow and in Spring it is a torrential river, but in the Summer and Fall it is a spectacular hike, indeed. It takes about four to six hours to walk down to the South Coast and about twice that to hike up, depending on one's physical condition and/or motivation. The only other way our or in is by the small carless ferry boat which services the small tourist village at the foot of the gorge. The natural beauty of the sheer rocky cliffs and the virgin forest is truly breathtaking, and swimming on the black sand beach is a fitting reward for the strenuous and exceptionally hot trek down the gorge. About halfway down the trail stands the deserted village of Samaria, while high on the hill above the Libyan Sea an ancient Venetian fortress guards the entrance to the gorge.

I doubt if I could count up the number of times I have been through the Samaria Gorge, yet each time is as if it were the first. The cool, pure air and fresh, pine smell at the top of the trail always bring back childhood memories of days spent hiking in the mountains near my home in the Pacific Northwest. Also, one never forgets the sheer presence of the huge boulders or the intense heat in the gorge's river bed. Several times we have seen wild mountain goats balancing on the rocks above us, both inquisitive and wary. This hike is always a

Samaria Gorge

highlight in the memories of the students and friends who share Crete with us. The fact that the gorge is now regulated by the government as a National Park should preserve its unique beauty and wonder.

At the very center of the island of Crete stands Mt. Ida, or "Psiloritis" as it is known by the native Cretans. It is the highest peak on Crete, some 7,500 feet, and has figured prominently into its geography and history. Ever since reading in Kazantzakis' quasi-autobiography, Report to Greco, about his own pilgrimage to the top of this mountain, I had hoped to do likewise. On the last day of July in 1981 I did so. There are three main routes up Psiloritis and I chose to go up the Western side from the Village of Fourfouras. The plan was to find a room in this village for the nights before and after the climb, but it happened that a wedding was taking place that day and every bed was already spoken for. A village of 300 people had suddenly grown to around 500. During the afternoon quite a number of people ambled through the central courtyard where I was sitting by myself under a large tree. One young man had lived in America for several years and was pleased to be able to freshen up his English. When asked where the trail to Psiloritis was, he replied that the best way to go was just across the road, down by the sheep gate.

Later on that day a number of young boys befriended me, and they too were glad to practice their schoolroom English. They took me to the church where we witnessed the conclusion of the wedding. The large patio outside the church was absolutely jammed with people singing and watching the bride and groom dance their first dance as a married couple. The reception began around 6 P.M. and lasted far into the night. After a huge meal, in which everyone participated, there was dancing, singing, and drinking. The boys guided me through the entire occasion. It was a real privilege, as a stranger, to be included in this celebration. It demonstrated, once again, the fact that in Crete the same word, "Zenos,' means both "stranger" and "guest." The introduction of the word "tourist" has, unfortunately, confused the issue considerably. There is no tourism whatsoever in mountain villages like Fourfouras.

The night was spent on the roof of a vacant building, half conscious of the wailing strains of bpuzuki music, which finally died out around 3 A.M. After a breakfast of leftovers from the feast of the previous evening, I stowed my backpack in an empty room, and crossed the road, and followed the path to the foot of the mountain. It was 6 A.M. It turned out that while this was, indeed, the most direct route to the top, it was also the most difficult. The various goat trails zig-zagged their way up between trees and boulders endlessly. Fortunately, this approach was on the Western side, so there was plenty of shade until about 10 o'clock when I finally clamored onto a large plateau used for grazing sheep. Across the plateau stood the final climb to the summit, a huge treeless, hillside covered with large rocks about the size of bowling balls. This turned out to be the hardest part of the journey, partly because the rocks tended to shift about when climbed on, but mostly because the air was getting much thinner by now.

The summit finally revealed itself at high noon. There really are no words with which to describe the view from the top of Psiloritis. To be able to see both the northern and southern coastlines, to recognize various towns and landmarks, all of which had previously been experienced separately, in one huge, panoramic view was absolutely exhilarating. When coupled with the sense of accomplishment that accompanies such a climb, this exhilaration became almost overpowering. I stood for a long time simply drinking in all that lay below. Eventually, however, the need to be drinking water asserted itself, and I began consuming as much of the remaining winter snow as I could possibly hold. It seemed a fitting and sufficient reward for my efforts.

The path down the South slope of the mountain led through woodlands, pastures, and finally olive groves and grape fields. After four hours it deposited my wobbly legs in a village 10 kilometers from Fourfouras. When I had downed three or four Coca-Colas at a local cafe, the owner offered to drive me back to my "base-camp." A whole watermelon served as an excellent appetizer for the evening meal and the hard rooftop seemed downright comfortable to an exhausted body. The early morning bus brought me down to the coast in time to spend most of the day soaking up the sun on the Rethymnon beach. Aching bones stimulated vivid images of yesterday's unforgettable adventure. Although unforgettable, this experience need not be unrepeatable. In fact, Mari and I are planning to climb Psiloritis together this coming summer.

The climbing of Psiloritis came at an important juncture in my own psychological development. For this reason it will always serve as a symbol or kind of spiritual landmark of what I experienced as my own "coming of age" as an independent person. I was nearing fifty and had been nearly devastated by the break-up of two marriages. I found it extremely difficult to function as a complete person on my own, outside of a relationship. Coming to Greece by myself for a whole summer represented a unique challenge in my growth as an individual. Climbing Psiloritis came at the conclusion of this summer on my own and served as the capstone of the entire experience. Mari and I met shortly after my return from this visit to Crete, so our climbing the mountain together will be a celebration of unity born out of strength rather weakness.

Cretan Sunset

Santorini View

There are two other islands, Santorini and Mikonos, that are part of the weave of my ongoing romance with Crete. Drawing near to Santorini by ship is a breathtaking as approaching Crete is sentimental. At a distance it looks much the same as the other Cycladic Islands, tan a treeless, rocky mass rising up out of the sea. As the ship swings into the huge inner bay, however, the sight of the sheer, thousand foot cliff with two snow white villages perched on top fills a person with pure awe. This mysterious quality of the island's appearance might make one wonder if he or she had somehow slipped into the world of science fiction. In spite of the power of tourism on this island, thanks at least in part to American Express advertisements, it is the almost overwhelming force of its vast, natural "presence" which engulfs and remains with those who visit there. In a word, it is the majesty of the place which attracts and lingers in the mind.

The view from the top of the cliff is every bit as splendid, though it is more romantic than overpowering. Santorini is a part of the remains of the caldera of the gigantic volcanic mountain that exploded around 1470 B.C., sending earthquakes, tidal waves, and soot-filled clouds throughout the southeastern Mediterranean and triggering the downfall of the Minoan civilization centered on

Santorini Sunset

Crete. The remaining island, along with its smaller sister island five miles or so across the bay, was resettled thousands of years ago, with several villages situated precariously on the rim of the caldera. In the center of the bay sits a tiny islet, the tip of the volcano itself, which continuously gives off sulphured steam. Santorini is a <u>live</u> volcano, and though it lies dormant most of the time, there have been at least two minor eruptions in this century. Tourists are allowed, indeed encouraged, to visit this small crater. This combination of surrounding islands coupled with the incredibly deep blue water, yields a fantastic, panoramic view at any time of the day. In the early morning hours there is a haunting stillness and at sunset the entire scene is at

Santorini View

once intensely real and unreal.

The gradually sloped backside of Santorini is covered with grape orchards and dotted with villages. There are exotic black and red sand beaches, and the wines from the islands vineyards are world famous. The volcanic fallout rendered the soil extremely fertile, even though the island has virtually no ground water source. While the main town of Fia boasts many high-class jewelry and fur stores, along with charming walking streets and fine restaurants, Santorini's, other villages offer an equally interesting, authentically Greek ambiance. This is especially true of the village of Ia, which is today what the main town of Fia once was, before it was "discovered" by tourism. Here one can still walk the streets, meeting more Greek than non-Greek people, and poke around in tiny shops and cafes. Here, too, one can literally hear the quiet of this mysterious island.

What primarily attracts me to Santorini, in addition to all of its

Santorini Akrotiri

romance and beauty, is the fact that it is the home of the largest active excavation of the Minoan civilization. Some 30 years ago a Greek archaeologist by the name of Marinatos theorized that there might well have been a Minoan outpost on the south coast of this, the nearest island to Crete. He began to dig near the present Village of Akrotiri. Sure enough, under more than 10 meters of volcanic ash, which fortunately is extremely light, he and his team discovered what has turned out to be an entire Minoan town. With only about one fourth of the excavation completed, several streets, with two and three-storied windowed houses, containing a number

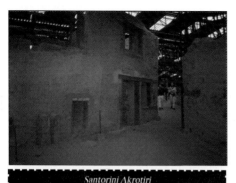

Santorini Akrotiri

of colorful morals and thousands of ceramic vases and large jars, have been uncovered. Since several palaces have been found on Crete, there remains a strong possibility that one will be discovered at the Akrotiri site.

It is an incredible experience to wander through the streets

Santorini Akrotiri

of this ancient town, peering in the windows and doors, imagining the Minoans of 4,000 years ago going about their daily routines. Now there is only the dusty silence of streets and stone stairways, broken by the earthquakes which destroyed this civilization a thousand years before the rise of what we know as a classical Greece. The murals and pottery taken from this excavation, now on display in the National Museum in Athens, are remarkably similar to those found at the palaces at Knossos and Festos on Crete. These latter have been exhibited in the Iraklion Museum for several decades. The Akrotiri dig continues throughout the summer months every year, directed by Marinatos' daughter, but funds for this sort of activity are never abundant.

One of the more remarkable facts about the excavation on Santorini is that the remains of not a single Minoan body have been unearthed. Unlike Pompei, where hundreds of people were taken by surprise by the eruption of nearby Mt. Vesuvius, their negative images preserved in the hardened volcanic ash, the Minoans living on Santorini seem to have left well before the final volcanic catastrophe took place. It is theorized that the serious character of the preeruption earthquakes served as ample warning, causing the complete evacuation from the island. It is possible that people in boats would have escaped the effects of the gigantic tidal wave caused by the eruption, which is estimated to have been 200 feet high when it reached Crete, since such waves travel underneath the water until forced to rise by a land mass. However, it is doubtful that any escapees in boats would have survived the hale of volcanic material which would have fallen for miles around.

Ironically, then, the only grave that one encounters while exploring the ruins at Akrotiri is that of professor Marinatos himself. About 20 years ago, while actually engaged in archaeological activity, he fell from a wall in one of the houses being un-covered, hitting his

Marinatos' grave

head on a rock. It seems highly appropriate, if also rather sad, that he should be buried right in the midst of this amazing excavation, which is both the apex of his life's work and the current high point of Minoan archaeology. The significance and mysterious beauty of this ancient town at Akrotiri at least equals, it not supersedes, that of the remainder of the island. In combination, its ancient and contemporary dimensions make Santorini a truly unforgettable reality.

The only other Greek island engraved in my memory is that of Mikonos. In previous decades Mikonos served as the symbol of the idyllic life in the islands of Greece, complete with windmills, donkeys, and small, multi-colored fishing boats. In recent years it has become widely known as a fast-lane, liberated vacation spot, full of nightclubs, gay bars, and nude beaches. I came to Mikonos for neither of these alternatives; I came looking for my friend Bo. Having heard from a mutual friend that Bo, who had been a student of mine some twelve years before, had built a house on Mikonos and spent his summers there, I thought it a fine idea to look him up.

After having asked around town for an hour or so, I found someone who knew Bo and gave general directions as to the location of his house. It turned out that Bo, who is a protestant minister, was known on M/konos as "Pappas," which is the Greek term for a priest. The bus driver dropped me off at what seemed to be the right dirt side road, though it was impossible to be sure. The sun was high and hot, and although there were several cheese pies in my pack, I had not thought to bring water. Anyway, Bo would be sure to have something to drink. A couple of farmers indicated that I was on the right road, which soon turned into a two-way path. When I reached the sea, after about an hour or so, there was an older woman bathing with a small child. Asking for "Pappas," I was told that he lived on the other side of the nearby mill. The climb over the hill was easy enough, and there in a beautiful sandy cove, all white and alone, stood Bo's house. It did not take long, however, to discover that he was not at home.

It was a lovely little one-room house, furnished with simple Greek furniture and a marvelous view. Waiting for Bo was a pleasant task. Swimming, sunbathing, and some napping took up the whole afternoon. The cheese pies silenced the hunger pangs but not the escalating thirst. There was not a well to be seen anywhere. I decided to climb up on the roof to wait for Bo, and if necessary spend the night there. Sleep came easily, but was interrupted in the middle of the night by the sound of nocturnal fisherman banging the side of his boat in order to attract fish. He also had a bright light with which to spot the fish, should they show up. Dawn came, but Bo did not. The note I left on the door read: "I came, I saw, I was conquered." By now the thirst was intolerable. The hike up to the road was uneventful if you do not count the viper which coiled and hissed when my boot nearly stepped on it. This was, by the way, the only poisonous snake I have ever encountered in Greece.

Since the social climate on M/konos was quite unattractive, the only real option was to go home to Crete as fast as possible. The plane ticket was easy to come by, but the plane itself was a different matter. The daily plane to Crete was broken, and its replacement would not arrive from Athens for several hours. Nine hours later we took off for Iraklion. The wait at the Mikonos airport proved fortuitous, however, for there stood Bo! He had come there to see another friend off, and we recognized each other instantly. So, for the better part of the nine-hour wait we visited about old times and new times. Bo loves Mikonos as much as I love Crete. We had a grand time sharing stories about our many Greek friends and adventures. Throughout our time together I consumed several large bottles of ice cold beer. When I blamed my prodigious thirst on his not having beer home, Bo paid for all my drinks, as any good Greek host would.

Over the years my many visits to Athens have all orbited around the Hotel Akropolis House, situated on the edge of both the Plaka (Old Athens) and Synlagma Square (Constitution Square). In addition to its extremely convenient location and its old world, family atmosphere, the chief attraction of the Akropolis House is the friendly attitude of the folks who operate it. Panos and his mother are, unsurprisingly, from Crete. We have been friends since my first visit to Greece over 20 years ago. They always provide special rates and room arrangements for our students, as well as a home-like atmosphere. We were there the night Greece won the European basketball championship, beating the Soviet Union in the finals, and everyone watched the games on television in the sitting room. We all celebrated together, along with the entire city of Athens, well into the morning hours of the next day.

From the Akropolis House nearly everything is within easy walking distance: the Parthenon, the flea market, the subway, the palace and parliament buildings, the major museums, and Lykavitos, the high hill from which one can enjoy a complete panoramic view of the entire city, including Piraeus the Athenian harbor town. The latter is a typical dirty, bustling port, full of commercial, military and industrial ships and trucks, small shipping agencies, and cheap hotels and taverns. In recent years it has also become a center for a great deal of illegal traffic, involving both substances and aliens from all over the world. Once the small bag containing our groups' plane tickets, travellers cheques, and my passport was stolen while we were waiting in Piraeus for the ship to Crete. The theft was so smooth that no one even knew it had taken place until about an hour later. Hopefully, we live and learn!

There are three excursions outside of Athens the memories of which remain especially vivid. One is to Delphi where the spectacular ruins of the religious center of classical Greece are located. The small contemporary town of Delphi is essentially a tourist spot, traditionally for the ruins and recently for skiers of the famous Mt. Parnasis. The ruins, which virtually hang on various levels of the steep and rocky cliff side, are among the most impressive in the world. Below the main road stands the partially reconstructed circular monument of Athena, along side of the large gymnasium area. Just above the road begins the processional entrance to the temple of Apollo, lined with shrines and treasures of all the major cities of the classical era. The huge foundation of the temple itself dominates the landscape, and its few standing pillars give mere hint of its previous size and stature. It was in the inner sanctum of this temple that the famous oracle of Delphi uttered its cryptic prophecies and judgments.

Directly above the temple stands the ancient and beautiful amphitheater, overlooking the temple and the entire valley below. Finally, at the top, are the remains of the sports stadium, complete with stone grandstand, starting blocks, and seats for dignitaries. Here was the center for the Pylphia Games, held every four years in the same fashion as the original games at Olympia. All wars were suspended and thousands of people came from all over Greece to pay tribute to their athletes, their cities, and their Gods. Delphi was also the home of healing springs and potions, a kind of health spa attracting scores of visitors daily. Walking through these ruins, one can almost feel the spiritual power emanating from the majestic hillside and the ancient stones. Delphi is a place and a presence not easily forgotten.

Two interesting stories about the Delphic Oracle are worth mentioning before moving on. It is said that an important general wanted to know if it was wise for him to go to war with one of his enemies. The Oracle said, "If you go to battle there will be a great victory." When the general, after having been soundly thrashed by his enemy, returned and complained to the temple priests, they pointed out that the Oracle had not specified whose victory it would be. Equally as ironic was the Oracle's reply to the query made by one of Socrates' friend as to whether anyone was wiser than he. "No one" came back the answer. Socrates himself, as a result of having repeatedly failed to prove the Oracle wrong by questioning self-proclaimed wiseman, concluded the Oracle simply meant to point out that Socrates was the wisest only because he alone would admit his ignorance. It would seem that even the Gods find it useful to hedge their bets.

Another significant excursion outside of the Athens area is that to Olympia. Throughout my childhood and youth I was extremely active in sports, especially track and field, and thus I had an uncommon interest in the Olympic Games. Indeed, one of my early dreams had been to compete in the Olympics as a long jumper. For these reasons, being able to visit Olympia was a highly exciting event. Like in Delphi, the contemporary villages is essentially a tourist stop, composed almost exclusively of small hotels, shops, and restaurants. The ruins, along with an excellent museum, are spread out over a large meadow-like area, which radiates a sense of peace and nostalgia. The temple of Zeus, toppled by an earthquake two thousand years ago, still exudes an imposing energy, as do the various shrines and treasures.

The entrance to the stadium has been paretically restored, so that one can enter the arena area through a small archway, as did the athletes in ancient times. Although the simple stadium itself is not particularly impressive, consisting of slightly raised grassy hillsides surrounding the relatively small playing field, the aura provided by its historical and cultural significance is amazingly tangible. Walking under the archway into the stadium, I tried to imagine the dramatic and festive atmosphere that must have filled this arena 2,500 years ago. I felt the butterflies in my stomach and could almost hear the cheering crowd. It was, of course, necessary for an ex-Olympic fantasizer to jog a lap around the stadium, drinking in the real and imagined glory. Afterwards I sat on a large stone in the sun for over an hour, soaking up the feel of that sacred place.

Yet a third important excursion is the trip to Epidaurus, the most well preserved and acoustically magnificent outdoor theater in all of Greece. Throughout the summer months the Greek National Theater sponsors the production of classic drama, in Greek, in this partially restored amphitheater. The great works of the Athenian playwrites can be experienced here, against the background of the waning sunset and the starry sky. The theater holds up to 14,000 people, all of whom can hear the theatrical whispers of the actors and coins falling on the stone floor. On a recent visit, my wife Mari, stood at center stage and sang for the small tourist audience. She said that the incredible acoustics brought her voice back to her own ears so clearly and forcefully that her singing was simply carried along by the song itself.

One of the plays I attended at Epidaurus was "The Bacchai." The tragic story of a mother and her friends, intoxicated by the power of their God Dionyssius, ripping her son's body apart, is truly terrifying. The set for the play consisted of huge, stone-like body parts strewn around the circular stage area. The drama unfolded as the characters moved about amongst the various parts of the set, creating a deeply haunting, and morbid effect. When the point was reached where the mother awakens from her trance and realizes what she has done, she uttered the loudest, most piercing cry of agony I have ever heard. The terror of this moment, multiplied by the grandeur of the setting, was astoundingly interrupted by the hilarious laughter of the huge, almost exclusively Greek audience.

I was completely dumbfounded and not a little angry at the insensitivity of the crowd. Walking back to the parking lot, I asked a young Greek friend why the people had burst out laughing at the most crucial moment of this famous and moving tragedy. I suggested that perhaps it was a release of nervous tension. He replied, however, that the vast majority of those who attend these plays know little or nothing about classical Greek drama, that they come to Epidaurus for a quiet family picnic and the theater. Moreover, few of them understand the ancient Greek language very well. In his opinion, most of the people were not following the play at the moment of the electrifying scream and it simply startled them and struck them as humorous.

Thessalonoki, the large, beautiful seaside capital of Northern Greece, lies about midway between the country's two most famous mountains, Mt. Olympus and Mt. Athos. Thus the room in the small, side street hotel would serve as convenient base camp for an encounter with both mountains, each for its own reasons. Thessalonoki itself is much cleaner and quieter than Athens, and the surrounding mountain sides are covered with evergreen trees. Here, too, is an excellent museum, the home of many recent and highly significant archaeological discoveries from the empire established by Philip of Macadonia, the father of Alexander the Great. It was Philip who hired the multi-talented philosopher Aristotle to be Alexander's childhood tutor. Aristotle, who also came from Macedonia, studied for 20 years with Plato in his "Academy" before opening his own school, called the "Lyceum."

Mt. Athos is a small mountain on the end of a peninsula, just up the coast from Thessalonoki. The peninsula which takes its name from the mountain, has been the home of about 20 monasteries of Orthodox Christianity for more than 800 years, during which time no women have been allowed in the area. The monastic communities maintain their own customs officials, have no towns, and are connected only by small donkey trails. Over the centuries these monasteries have housed thousands of monks, who have been the chief preservers of the Orthodox faith of eastern Europe, Greece and Russia through times of great difficulty and oppression. Today most of these communities are defunct, the buildings standing as silent reminders of the glory and riches of Medieval Christianity. A few of the monasteries are, however, not only open but are thriving. Having heard of Mt. Athos during my theological studies, and having read Kazantzakis' account of his visit to its monasteries, I was eager to experience this unique place first-hand.

After obtaining official permission to make a four day pilgrimage on the holy peninsula, it is necessary to wait one's turn in the little village of Ouranopolis (heavenly city) before being taken into the area of the monasteries by small boat. No radios, cameras, or short pants were allowed. It seemed best to plan to spend all four days in one monastery, rather than hopping around, since this would provide a better understanding of what life on Mt. Athos is really like. Having been given minimal directions to the monastery called "Filoutheou" (Friend of God), I set out on what proved to be about a 10 kilometer trek along beautiful, but poorly marked and rather steep trails. After several hours Filoutheou rose up before me like a medieval fortress at the top of the next hill.

The official "greeter" at the main gate, a smiling young monk with the beginnings of a scraggly beard, led the way to a cool waiting room where fresh water and "Turkish Delight" candies were provided. I signed the guest book and was led to a small dormitory room containing a single bed and a chair, directly across the hall from the common toilet and shower room. The monastery was designed as a rectangle of four large, continuously joined buildings, which housed the dormitory, dining hall, library, storerooms, and "offices." In the center of the inner courtyard stood a lovely chapel. There were about 50 monks living at Filoutheou, most of whom were quite young, and several older priests, who were very obviously in charge of things. As would be expected, it was extremely quiet at all times.

The simple but ample vegetarian supper was eaten in silence, and was followed by a brief scripture reading and prayer. Afterward I spoke with an energetic, middle-aged monk, whose English was excellent, about my desire to enter into the life of the monastery as thoroughly as possible. He informed me that worship took place at 1:30 A.M. and that the next day we would make soap together. Everyone went to bed at sundown, and I fell into a very deep sleep. A brisk knock on the door announced that it was time for worship, and through the window could be seen a long line of monks carrying candles into the chapel. Only then did I realize that the monastery operated entirely without electricity. The worship lasted about an hour and a half and consisted exclusively of scripture, prayer, and continuous Gregorian-like chanting. We sat in high straight backed, wooden chairs all around the outside walls of the chapel. The candlelight cast a mysterious yet comforting glow throughout the room, and the chanting was deeply moving.

Making soap took all day and involved mixing the vegetable fat collected in the kitchen together with a specific chemical compound, in a huge vat over an extremely hot wood fire. After a few hours of cooking and stirring, the soap was poured into large, three-inch deep flats where, after it hardened, it was cut up into hand-sized chunks, each of which was stamped with the image of an eagle. The chunk of Filoutheou soap, which has sat on the mantle at home for over ten years now, serves as a fond reminder of that hard, hot, but fascinating day working side by side with a dedicated yet shrewd monk. When asked if the monks study any theology, he replied that while the purpose of theology would appear to be the enhancement of spiritual life, here at the monastery it was possible to grow spiritually through work and prayer. "therefore, we do not need theology."

Although I was tempted to quibble with him over this narrow understanding of both theology and spiritual life, I thought better of it. In addition to the goal of spiritual development of the individual monks, the monasteries see themselves both as centers of prayer for the world and as examples to it. Even though I respect the motivations of this approach to religious faith, as well as the immense value of the simple life within a self-sufficient community, I confess that I think it would be more effectively applied through greater direct involvement with the world that it seeks to serve. There is a great deal of good work that can be done, and only done, at the specific places of special need, as Mother Theresa has so clearly demonstrated. Moreover, the example of the simple life being set for the world to imitate needs to be lived where it can be seen, not cloistered away where it is perhaps a bit too shelter ed for those already in it and too hidden from those who most desperately need it. In short, it is difficult for me to imagine Jesus living in a monastery.

The next day was spent in the kitchen washing dishes and praticing my Greek with the monks working there. This task was far more familiar than making soap, and these young men were somehow less serious or "officious" than the others. The ritual of silent meals, retiring at dusk and rising for prayer at 1:30 A.M. and rising again at 6 A.M for the work day had a very stabilizing yet energizing effect. Also, the beautiful setting and weather exuded a most peaceful setting and health-giving aura. During the evenings I was reading an interesting book, which one of the monks gave me, on the history and practice of Orthodox Christianity. It had split off from Western, Roman Catholicism around 1000 A.D. over the questions of the absolute authority of the Pope and whether the Holy Spirit flows from God the Father with Christ the Son, or indirectly through Christ the Son. Over the centuries this branch of the Christian church has remained far more democratic, much less powerful politically, and a great deal more esoteric and mystical than its Western counterpart.

On the morning of my last day at the monastery, my soap-making supervisor asked me if I would spend the day watering the fruit orchard, as he himself had to visit another monastery on some business. The long, large plastic hose was implanted in the nearby stream and as long as it was laid out in a downhill fashion there was plenty of water for watering. The orchard was surrounded by a forest of slender chestnut trees, indigenous to Mt. Athos, which begin to grow again as soon as they are cut down. All of the monasteries are maintained largely by money received from selling this self-perpetuating resource to local lumber companies. Fortunately, these loggers work individually and with donkeys rather from trucks, so the peacefulness of the countryside is not much disturbed by their presence.

That evening, as I was resting on a wall outside the entrance to the monastery, my supervisor rode up on the donkey. "Did you do it?," he asked, referring to the watering of the orchard. "Yes," I replied. "Need I check?," with a sly grin. "No," I answered, and he rode on through the gate. A man of few words, but not without feeling. For the next morning, as I prepared to leave, he met me outside the gate with a helpful little map of the best route back to the return boat and a special gift. Out of his robe he produced one of his monk hats, about six inches high and made of black velvet. He explained that while priests hats have a small hip around the top, monk's hats do not. "God's speed," he smiled, and disappeared back through the gate. The hat gets worn, along with an academic gown, twice a year at college festivities. In addition to looking much more regal and feeling far more comfortable, the hat puts me in remembrance of four highly significant days spent on Mt. Athos.

Though distinctively different from a visit to Mt. Athos, an encounter with Mt. Olympus offers a challenge and a significance all its own. The traditional home of Zeus and the other Gods of Greek mythology, Mt. Olympus is the tallest peak in all of Greece. It seemed a fitting conclusion to these solitary journeys through the matrix of Western culture to pay my respects by climbing its highest and most important summit. It turned at that there is a right way and a wrong way to go about this adventure. The next time I undertake this challenge, I shall remember to do it the right way. It is not a difference in propriety or anything like that; its simply a matter of being sensible or not being sensible.

The bus from Thessaloniki dropped me off in the small village at the base of Mt.Olympus around noon. Feeling fit and a bit adventuresome, I set off up the road toward the top.Every now and then a full car or taxi would pass by, and since they nearly all returned empty, it was safe to assume that they were depositing hikers at the beginning of the actual trail leading to the summit. After an hour or so it became obvious that the whole afternoon could be spent wasting time walking on this road. It was a simple matter to get one of the empty taxis to turn around and take me the 5 kilometers to the tourist pavilion where the official hike up Mt.Olympus begins. It was now around 2 P.M. After registering with the National Park Guide, I began my pilgrimage once again. So much for the wrong way of approaching this adventure.

The climb was every bit as beautiful as it was steep. The backpack, which should have been left in a rented room in the village, began to get very heavy. Several times donkeys passed by, carrying supplies as well as their master to the hiker lodge near the top. The forest was so thick that only occasionally could one catch a glimpse of the coastline far below. I noticed an anthill and distracted myself for 20 minutes or so by contemplating the fact that they were not even aware that they were hiking on the side of one of the world's most famous mountains. Just after I began to wonder if I was going to make it to the lodge before the increasing darkness was complete, I found myself staggering up its steps. The climb had taken 5 hours.

The lodge was full of friendly people, all busily engaged in having supper. The man in charge said he had room for one more, both at the table and on the floor in the long sleeping loft above the dining room area. It turned out that about 50 of the 80 people staying at the lodge overnight were members of a Greek hiking club, most of whom were high school teachers, all of whom spoke excellent English. When the after dinner conversation got around to politics, things heated up a good deal. Although this is generally the case all over the world, it is especially typical in Greece. Some say that arguing about politics is the Greek national pastime.

Anyway, at one point in the discussion one of the male teachers threw up his hands and announced that he was tired of speaking about such important matters in English. "If you want to talk to me about these things, you will have to learn enough Greek to do so. Why should we always have to be the ones who must learn a foreign language before real conversation can take place?" I fell asleep that night pondering his discomforting question. Just why do English speaking people assume that everyone else in the world will and should learn to speak English? Perhaps its a matter of both laziness and arrogance on our part.

In the morning only a middle-aged German couple and myself were headed toward the summit, all the others, having completed their climb the day before, were on their way down the mountain. The lodge was situated about 1,000 feet from the peak, all but the last hundred yards or so being a relatively easy climb though a steep meadow area. Near the peak we were confronted by a huge pile of gigantic boulders on which the way to the very top was marked with large dots of red paint. The German couple declared that they were not going up there without ropes, and turned back. Since I had come this far and was now so close, I was determined to go on.

The climb up the boulders was a bit tricky, but I was soon at the highest spot. The swirling winds were incredibly strong and it was necessary to hold on very tightly in order to scan the panorama of the vast countryside spread out below in every direction. Suddenly I was enveloped in a thick fog for the first time felt genuinely afraid. The red spots became visible one at a time as I groped my way back down off the boulders. Although it may have been a unwise decision, especially since I was alone, I was and remain glad that I pushed myself to the summit of Mt. Olympus. There are some things more important than safety.

The trip down the trail took only three hours and was easy, except that it is extremely dangerous to ramble down a mountain side on legs made of jello. It would hardly have been surprising to find myself flat on my face on the rocky path several times over, but Zeus must have been smiling on me. I have no memory of the bus ride back to Thessalonoki, but I shall always remember lying in a tub of cold, not hot, water for over an hour at the hotel. The need to be revived outweighed the need to sooth the complaining muscles. The lengthy soak provided an excellent opportunity to savor this dramatic finale to my less than Homeric journeys through Greece.

Chapter Three
A New Home in Sitia

Throughout our years of visiting Crete we had become somewhat familiar with the town of Sitia, just an hour or so east of Mochlos. When it came time to make concrete arrangements for the semester in Greece program, we decided to situate it in Sitia. We knew and preferred the eastern end of Crete, but Mochlos is clearly too small and isolated for an educational enterprise of this size and duration. So, during the last one month tour we came to Sitia several times to get a better sense of the place and to arrange for rental housing. For the students we located a small, extremely quaint and well preserved hotel run by a fellow named Apostolis. For ourselves we found a lovely tri-plex apartment about five kilometers east of town along the coast road.

Early June of the following year found us along with a great deal of luggage, on the morning bus from Iraklion to Sitia, full of excitement and no small amount of trepidation. The plan was to live here on our own for three months and continue on for another 3 months after the students arrived in September. This was surely the biggest adventure of our lives. Sitting directly behind us on the bus was a young woman returning home from the University of Iraklion. She was extremely friendly, spoke excellent English, and her name Elpida, means "Hope" in Greek. She told us about her parents, both of whom were teachers, and her younger brother, Yanis. As the years have gone by we have become very good friends with this family. They have played an important role in helping us feel at home in Sitia.

When our landlord explained that he had taken the liberty of putting us in a different unit in his tri-plex, we were not sure what to think. When we had an opportunity to look the place over the next morning, we knew that the apartment would not work for us. Fortunately, a friend of Apostolis, yet another Yanis, arranged for us to look at another apartment, one which turned out to be much nicer, closer to town, and less expensive. The "Villa Romantsa" became our new home the very next day. We now had a flowered patio, a view of the sea, and three semi-domesticated cats. Our next door neighbors were a young couple, he a local Greek named Vangeli and she an Austrian named Ingrid.

Sitia is a lovely and friendly town, laid out on a curved hill side,

Sitia Evening

facing northeasterly. It has a long stretch of sandy beach, as well as a working harbor full of small fishing boats and occasional tourist and transport ships. The harbor is lined with several dozen taverns, restaurants, and discos. There is a partially restored Venetian fortress on the hill above the town, and many of the streets are actually wide and steep stairways because of the hillside on which Sitia is built. Since it is the last major stop along the coastal road, there are significantly fewer tourists than in other towns and cities in Crete. The citizens of Sitia number around 6,000, so there are several banks, good bus service, a large high school, and a new hospital. There is also a small supermarket, a lively, somewhat crowded downtown center, and a basketball team.

The weeks of the Summer were mostly spent writing, reading and swimming at the beach, and getting Mari set up to do her pottery. The days were long, hot, and very dry. Although there is usually a steady northwesterly breeze, it never rains in the summer on Crete. We often ate at one of the outdoor restaurants in the evening. In addition to providing excellent and inexpensive food, they gave us ample opportunity to enjoy the continuous parade of people up and down the promenade. Especially interesting were the local families, most of whom came out to eat often and late. They would begin to gather around 9 or 10 P.M.

and would linger until well past midnight, the children running and riding their bikes and trikes in the carless street. Even the town mascot, Nikos the four foot high pelican, loved to strut amongst the crowd.

Since I both enjoy playing basketball, and since it seemed like a likely way to get to know some folks in town, I began frequenting the community center's outside court and participating in some pick-up games with local high school boys. Soon I was invited to play when the "big boys" play, three evenings a week at 6 P.M. Even at this hour it was extremely hot and somewhat quite windy. In addition to having a fine time and getting to know a good number of local men, I also had the opportunity to pick up some basic Greek. The local men's team turned out to be excellent, and from this regular contact I made many friends. In fact, I became something of a celebrity, being by far the oldest player in town and an American as well. The interest in basketball among Greek young men is high, especially after the national team has done so well, and America still sets the standards in the sport.

The star and coach of the team was Yarv†nt, a large, seriously talented fellow with a bashful grin. He was in his early thirties and had played professional basketball in the top-level Athenian city league. Now he was teaching physical education at the high school and working in his family's shop in town, all in addition to his basketball duties. Yarvant's family is of Armenian descent and several years before he travelled with an ethnic team to play games in the Los Angeles area. The Sitia team usually finished in second place among the six team league on Crete, and consisted of a policeman named Vasili, a men's shoe store owner named Marco, Kosta, who had just returned from the Army, three fellows name Yorgos, and Stellios, a local civil engineer. There were also the high school boys who played on the men's team as well as on the school team, Dino and, yes another Yorgos.

Basketball, like all sports, is an excellent indicator of many aspects of Greek culture. Like Americans, for instance, Greek men participate in a healthy amount of minor controversy while playing in pick-up games without official referees. However, the latter engage in verbal disputes throughout officiated games as well, and even escalate them into full-scale dramatic events. At the first game of the season in September, we were amazed, confused, and greatly entertained by the amount and intensity of the histrionics permitted. Every major judgment of the referees was hotly disputed, with arm-waving, verbal abuse, and threatening gestures abounding. It took nearly twice as long to complete the game as one would normally expect. Nevertheless, not only were there no incidents of actual physical confrontation, but all of this hoopla was simply taken in stride by everyone present. It was all part of the Greek, or at least Cretan way.

The same phenomenon could be observed at the football, or soccer matches. Sitia also had an excellent team in this more traditional sport, attracting several hundred supporters at every game. Here, however, the crowd sometimes became downright abusive, especially of the referees. More than once they were chased by spectators and had to be protected by the police. This is something of a world-wide phenomenon in this sport, especially in Mediterranean and Latin American countries, but by no means limited to them. Fortunately, things do not get carried to such extremes in basketball, even in Greece. In fact, the Greek National Team is particularly noted for its serious, yet sportsman-like conduct.

Reflecting on these behavior patterns, especially within the specific context of basketball games in Sitia, has brought me to two somewhat conflicting conclusions. To begin with, there is a sense of grassroots, participatory democracy at work in these contests, something stemming perhaps from the classical Greek belief that everyone is entitled to an explanation for every decision and each person has a right to have their say. Thus the referees, like politicians, must justify all of their major judgments to the satisfaction of those involved. While ideally this approach makes a great deal of sense, it is not, as Plato and Aristotle clearly saw, very conducive to efficiency. It can easily deteriorate into anarchy. At the same time, however, when participants acquiesce too quickly to official decisions, totalitarianism is generally the result.

Secondly, it is interesting, and perhaps instructive, to speculate on how significant this tendency toward violent disputation in athletic contests is with regard to the prospects for world peace. On the surface it might seem like a trivial thing in contrast to the apparent progress toward world community that has been made in recent years, especially in the disintegration of the Soviet Union and the unification of Western Europe. However, it is nonetheless troubling that at that fundamental level of local athletic contests, people around the world remain so ferociously competitive and territorial. It is difficult to imagine how real progress toward world unity and peace can take place until these ethnic and nationalistic tendencies are overcome or at least more productively sublimated.

One of the Yorgoses on the basketball team is the youngest of three brothers whose family owns the Krystal hotel in downtown Sitia. That first Summer he and I spent many hours on the court together and became close friends. Over the years that our college program has been operating in Sitia, Yorgos and his family have been extremely kind and helpful to our students, and Yorgos himself has even visited them and us in American. He has spent several years studying and working in Paris, and speaks French as well as English fluently. During the first week of September, Yorgos always invites our freshly arrived students to the outdoor celebration of his birthday. In addition to providing us with this opportunity to meet many local young people and enjoy an abundant offering of excellent Greek food, Yorgos also entertains us by singing and playing his guitar.

Mari's main concern that first summer was organizing her ceramic activity. Our apartment patio offered an excellent corner for a studio set-up, but both clay and a throwing wheel had to be acquired. It turned out that the same man who found us our apartment also ran an art shop in Sitia and a pottery along the coastal road a bit further east of town. He made some phone calls and located a company in Athens which would ship a first-rate Japanese wheel from Crete. The complex bureaucracy indigenous to Greece, intensified by the recent Socialist regime, made its presence felt in connection with this transaction, as well as with the many boxes of books we had sent to ourselves for the program's library. In both cases there were many forms to be filled out, extra money to be paid, and a good of general confusion.

There is a grand opportunity for learning patience while trying to adjust to life in a less technologized culture. Not being able to keep one's place in line, since there are no lines, or to find out exactly when, or even if, a certain bus or boat is departing, can be infuriating to a person who lives in a "modernized" society. It is especially difficult when one is a highly organized and somewhat impetuous person, like myself, and is trying to co-ordinate a dependable study program for a group of twenty. Nevertheless, by allowing twice as much time as one normally would for all business transactions, and by reminding oneself that speed and efficiency are not the only important values in life, a great deal of anxiety can be avoided and a large amount of patience can be learned.

There is a definite village atmosphere that pervades Cretan culture, lying just beneath the modernized, technological surface. The streets in Sitia, for instance, were nearly all made before the arrival of the automobile and are very narrow. This makes traffic extremely congested and noisy, but people still maintain the upper-hand by simply insisting on walking

Sitia Street Scene

in the streets. The cars and trucks must negotiate their way through the city with great care and little speed. There is a directness of action and speech here that characterizes even city life, a directness which often startles and confuses the visitor. People greet each ther and carry on business across large spaces, whether on the street or in the bank, and they walk straight to their destination with little regard for traffic, whether motorized or on foot. This may seem like a strange way to do business, but it does help maintain a more humane, personable way of life.

One place where this direct, village-like made of existence is highly detrimental is on the highway. In towns like Sitia there a

Cretan Village Life

number of stop signs, but no traffic lights, while the surrounding roads for the most part are narrow and not well marked. The local people, farmers, merchants, and young people alike, generally drive as if no one else is on the road. Not only do they go too fast and pass in extremely unsafe spots, but they frequently come around blind corners on the wrong side of the road. If it as if the significance of the difference between cars and trucks, on the one hand, and donkeys and carts, on the other hand, has not yet fully dawned on them. Traffic deaths in Greece, especially among "dare devil" young people, constitute a major social problem. Bus drivers, fortunately, are extremely well-trained and careful, even though it sometimes appears that they take their vehicles where no bus could or should ever go.

While we are on the subject, let me mention one other major area where the village attitude continues to express itself, even though the consequences of technology demand a change. For many, many centuries the people of Crete have produced waste which has been exclusively biodegradable. The sun and the salt sea disposed of all garbage quite naturally. With the introduction of various kinds of plastic, as well as the abundance of other petroleum and metallic products, however, all that has changed. Unfortunately, the village mentality toward waste has not kept pace with environmental pollution, and only recently have instituted programs for collecting and disposing of unbiodegradable waste products. Consequently, one encounters a good deal of garbage, trash, and cast-away mechanical devices cluttering up the otherwise beautiful landscape.

Now, to get back to where we left off, the procuring of clay for Mari's pottery projects was far easier and far more enjoyable than obtaining a potter's wheel. In fact, here all of the positive aspects of the Cretan village mentality forcefully exerted themselves. Through yet another Yorgos, this time the operator of one of the many Kiosks in town, we learned of an excellent potter working full-time in the mountain village of Mirsini, not far from Mochlos. Incidentally, a Kiosk, termed a "Pereeptero" in Greek, a uniquely European phenomenon, is a little stand which sells everything from magazines and newspapers to cigarettes, candy, soda pop, stamps, and toys. This Yorgos, who doubles as a singer of folk songs and whose wife is from Yugoslavia, also became our close friend and a help to our students. Anyway, we dispatched ourselves to Mirsini in search of Nikos the potter and perhaps some information about where to buy clay.

It turned out that the only source of potter's clay on Crete is a manufacturer living and working in Mires, on the southern coastal plain of Messara. However, Nikos the potter being as generous as he is amazing, was more than happy to sell, indeed almost give, Mari all she would ever need from his own supply. The real story here turned out to be Nikos himself. After high school, where incidentally he had played on the same basketball team with Yarvant and Stellios in Sitia, Nikos studied pottery in Athens for two years. Then, after a brief stint in Germany, he returned to his home village to set up his own studio and ceramics shop. Rather rapidly he has developed quite a successful enterprise, which includes his mother working away at the family's ancient loom to produce very beautiful shawls and rugs.

Nikos himself makes extraordinary vases, trays, and dinner sets, experimenting with a wide variety of shapes and glazes. He manages to sell a large number of pieces to tourists who stop by, either in response to Nikos' roadside signs or as a result of their vacation visit to the tourist hotel on the sea below, near

Mochlos. In fact, the view from Nikos' studio, of the entire sea coast surrounding and including Mochlos, may be the most astounding and beautiful in the entire area. It is the lights of Mirsini that folks in Mochlos see first, as dusk begins to fall in eastern Crete. Somehow this connection between Mochlos and Nikos, who often visits there himself, helps weave our current experience in Sitia into the pattern previously established by our visits to Mochlos.

Over the years Nikos has remained a close and enthusiastic friend, and in addition he and Mari have become colleagues in clay, continuously exploring and supporting each others work. She brings him books on ceramics from America and shares the latest knowledge acquired from her master-teacher there, while he explains his experiments with glazes and even refuses to take money when firing her pots in his large electric kiln. Whenever we go to visit Nikos, or whenever he comes to Sitia on his ancient BMW motorcycle, he always greets us by throwing his arms out, stamping his feet and lamenting: "Why you never call me?" When we do call him, we often get a chance to speak with his mother which gives us an opportunity to practice our limited Greek, as confusing as it often is.

Recently Mari has made contact with a local travel agent named Panayotis who also has a tourist gift shop. At his home Panayotis has an electric kiln which he allows her to use in exchange for displaying her vases and bowls on consignment in his shop. He himself knows quite a bit about the technological aspects of ceramics and occasionally even sells some of Mari's works. There remain, however, definite limitations with respect to the types of clay, glazes, and temperatures available for the serious potter on Crete. Specifically, the Cretan clay would not stand up to the sort of heat necessary to achieve the quality of glazing possible in a high fire kiln, even if one were available. Mari finds it challenging, nevertheless, to explore the possibilities offered within these limitations, during the months we are on Crete.

Throughout our first Summer in Sitia, our closest friend was Apostolis, the owner of the small hotel we had arranged for the students to live in during the coming fall semester. He helped us with the many details of getting settled in a new place, and we spent a number of evenings together at various tavernas swapping tales and arguing politics. It turned out that Apostolis'

Students in Sitia

hotel was too small and "refined" to work well as student living quarters and too near the noises and "temptations" of downtown Sitia for an educational center. After a good deal of discussion between ourselves, as well as with Apostolis, a mutual decision was reached to locate our program in a different place of following year. This turn of events put a good deal of strain on our relationship with Apostolis, but he has remained a good friend, nevertheless.

Our landlords at the Villa Romantsa, Yorgos and Kiki, both around 70 years of age, slowly became our closest friends in Sitia. He is a retired Toyota dealer and she a retired physical education teacher. In addition to managing two villas and handling the insurance needs of many local citizens, Yorgos also farms a large number of olive groves. Their daughter, Maria, together with

Villa Romantsa

her two small children, lives with her husband, Spiros, a military officer, in Alexandropolis, near Istanbul. Their 35 year old son, Nikos, lives at home, above his father's office, with his parents. Since childhood he has suffered from some sort of neurological disease which inhibits his speech and muscular behavior, but in no way inhibits his spirit. During the day he runs errands for his parents and at night he hangs out with the local taxi drivers. At all times, Nikos is enthusiastically friendly and in possession of an excellent sense of humor.

When I arose around 7 A.M. to get started on my writing projects, Yorgos would be weeding and watering in the flower garden directly in front of our windows. We would pass the time of day and practice our international greetings. We both knew about the same number of German and Italian words, and Yorgos' favorite English expressions are "Good Morning," "Excuse Me," and "Thank you very much." As he hustles around the villa taking care of business, Yorgos exhibits something of a comic or clownish character, but he is an exceedingly thoughtful and shrewd person as well. Although he has various aches, pains and ailments, he is incredibly active and agile physically, walking a lot and swimming nearly every day.

Since Mari and I both enjoy gardening, we slowly inherited much of the responsibility for weeding and watering. Indeed, now that we have situated our college program at the villa, and maintain our apartment year around, Yorgos has delegated quite a number of responsibilities to us. Quite a few special arrangements had to be made, as well, for such things as Mari's wheel, a telephone, and the arrival of students. Throughout this process, Yorgos learned to trust us, and we him, in an implicit and enjoyable manner. Even the financial arrangements concerning rent, electric bills, etc. have all been handled in a business-like, yet very informal fashion.

Slowly we have almost been brought within the family by Yorgos and Kiki. Not only have they taken us out to eat a number of times each year, but they have had us to their home several times for dinner and have given us many gifts of food, olive oil, and flowers. During our second summer in Sitia, they invited us to the baptism of their youngest grandchild. The baptismal service itself was long, highly ritualized, and joyous occasion for everyone, except of course for the child. Being stripped and immersed into a huge bowl of tepid water by a strangely talking man in stranger looking clothes and a long beard was clearly a frightful experience. The celebration after the baptism included great feasting and drinking, as well as ample opportunity to practice the few Greek

Traditional Cretan Dancers

dance steps we had been learning.

Space will not permit a full rundown of all of the friends we have made in Sitia, but a few more deserve mentioning. There is Eva, the young woman from whom we bought our small, black and white, made-in-China television. She is extremely typical of a great many Cretan young people today, who are raised in traditional, somewhat backward village communities and who now live and work in largely modernized towns and cities. Although she speaks both English and French, and is studying computer programming, hoping to move beyond the confines of Sitia, her strong root connections with her family and home village make her apprehensive about leaving the area. However, êva is clear that she will not marry early, or into a traditional, patriarchical marriage. This commitment also places her, along with a great many young Cretan women, a precarious position between her traditional past and her potential future. The expectations of the culture and men in Greece, especially outside of Athens, place sever limitations on today's young women.

Another young woman friend who is struggling to find a way to combine a meaningful marriage with a life of her own outside of the home is Melina. She owns a thriving bookstore in downtown Sitia and has been rather helpful to us and our students over the years. Like many other store owners, she often gives us gifts and almost always gives us discounts on everything we buy. In addition,

Melina not only places special book orders for us, but employed Tim our art student friend, to design and paint the large sign above the door of her store. Her young husband manages an athletic clothes store a few blocks away.

The last week of our first college program in Sitia we met a young Greek couple living quite near us in another villa. Peggy is an archaeologist working for the local museum at the Minoan excavation in nearby Palekastro and Nikos is a grade school teacher in a village a few miles away. Although they are typical of modern, well educated young Greek people in their interests and abilities, they are quite atypical in many of their valves and attitudes. To begin with, Peggy and Nikos prefer living in semirural Crete over metropolitan Athens or even Iraklion. Moreover, not only is Nikos different from most young men by virtue of having chosen to be a grade school teacher, but he is also very domestic. He cooks, does the dishes, and tends the garden. Peggy tutors in French and English in her spare time, as well as taking part in a local drama club. This past Summer it was a great pleasure to share in their enjoyment of their new born baby.

In addition to the regular pattern of exploring the many swimming and snorkeling beaches surrounding Sitia, we engaged in a regular shopping pattern as well. for packaged and miscellaneous goods the co-operative "supermarket" was least expensive and most well stocked. Aside from the fact that it is a bit disorganized, its chief drawback is that it is located over a kilometer up the road which leads down into town. Since we spent our first year in Sitia without a car, shopping there proved to be a rather major undertaking. The bus brought us to town, but after walking through town, up the hill, doing the shopping, and staggering down the hill with a half dozen heavy bags, the taxi was the favorite way of getting back home. After that first year, we acquired a volkswagen mini-van and shopping became a much more enjoyable proposition, both for us and for the students.

Shopping for fresh fruit, vegetables, and bread, however, was and is an inherently enjoyable undertaking. For such items are obtained from the various small, family run shops found along the busy streets of downtown Sitia. Here one gets to poke around among the flats and baskets for the freshest items, as well as greet and visit with a wide variety of shoppers and friends. Getting the best fruit and vegetables on any given day requires going to several different shops, while there are but two bread shops. The bread, however, comes directly from the bakery every morning, hot and wholesome. Most food on Crete costs about half of what it does in America, and this goes for the cost of eating at the harborside restaurants, as well. Along with various sorts of grilled fish and meat, delicious salads and stuffed vegetables abound, and everything is cooked in healthy, cholesterol-free olive oil.

Every Tuesday morning, along one of the major streets on the hill above the downtown area, a kind of "peoples market" takes place. Dozens and dozens of farmers, free-lance merchants, and hustlers display and peddle their wares on the street, out of their trucks, or along temporary tables. In addition to being colorful and interesting, even sometimes somewhat exotic, this market often offers useful and very inexpensive merchandise. Along with various kinds of fresh foods, there are all sorts of clothing items, sheets, blankets, flowers, kitchen gadgets and gizmos, and even live rabbits. It is fun just to walk, or rather squeeze, along the street amidst the crowd shopping, gawking, and people watching. The market opens at 6 A.M. and it is best to come early for the best bargains.

There is a relaxed, neighborly atmosphere about the shops and stores in Sitia, which makes shopping both interesting and pleasant. For the most part, people are friendly and helpful, without high pressure, hard-sell techniques and attitudes. After one becomes a regular customer, it is even more enjoyable to frequent the downtown area. Although the people of Sitia are used to seeing strangers, because during the summer months the town is crowded with them, they are not used to seeing them week after week, especially if they speak some Greek. The citizens are glad to see us and seem proud that foreigners both choose to live and work in their town and try to speak their difficult language.

Indeed, we receive a great deal of special treatment from various shopkeepers, including special prices. This makes us feel both honored and more than slightly embarrassed, since we not only have far more money than most of these folks, but we are never able to reciprocate. This does not seem to bother our friends, however, for they genuinely enjoy treating strangers as guests. There is, after all, but one word in Greek, Xenos, for what we in English separate into these distinct two categories. This, too, is one of the characteristics of the more traditional, village-like mentality that is rapidly being replaced by the technological and capitalistic aspects of modernity. In spite of all the personal and social drawbacks of the more "primitive" cultural climate, its simplifying and humanizing values far outweigh whatever advantages modernization can offer. Fortunately, Sitia is a place where such changes are fewer and slower than in many other places.

One other way in which this traditional Cretan hospitality has expressed itself in our life in Sitia pertains to my sculpting activities. Whenever the need for various materials with which to mount the sculptures arises, different folks in town prove to be more than co-operative. The men at the marble shops, for instance, are always glad to help with the drilling of the appropriate holes in the stone. Several of the local carpenters have been very helpful in providing and shaping wood bases, as well. None of these folks will ever take any money for such assistance; they simply smile and say: "Teepota" ("It's nothing"). Even the shoe repair shop refuses to accept payment for sewing up my sandals. Such humanity is not an easy thing to come by, except perhaps in Crete and other non-"civilized" places.

The conjunction of these two themes, shopping and traditional village attitudes, appears again in connection with yet another common Greek custom. Every afternoon at 2 P.M. nearly all markets and stores close for the afternoon siesta. Most people go home for a large mid-day meal and a lengthy nap, returning to reopen for business from 5 to 8 P.M. on Tuesday, Thursday, and Friday. Banks, most offices, and markets, do not reopen, while restaurants and the post office do not close for the afternoon. This staggered schedule, needless to say, makes it necessary to plan one's shopping and business rather carefully. The dozen or so taxis that wait in the town plaza are generally available from early morning straight through until midnight, although this pretty much depends on the discretion of each individual driver.

Which brings us directly to a larger issue. The siesta phenomenon reflects a general Greek, or at least Cretan, attitude toward the relationship between work and leisure. By and large, the traditional way of life approaches work, such as farming and fishing, as a way of making a living, as a means to an end. Even though the goal and the means are generally inextricably intertwined, most work is seasonal and the village mentality never allows the enjoyment of life to get lost in the striving with the means. Unlike Americans and northern Europeans, the Greek person has no difficulty closing up shop on a given day, or for an unscheduled period of days, simply because the weather, the fishing, the hunting, or family interests warrant it. A great deal of time is spent simply enjoying the good but simple things in life, including family and friends.

Although this more relaxed attitude toward work is, in itself, quite appealing, there is a down-side to it, as well. Dividing their lives equally between work and play, as it were, Greek people generally avoid the psychological and cultural dangers associated with the Western compulsion to turn even leisure into a kind of work. However, on the debit side, very little energy and time are spent by Greek people expanding their intellectual and creative capacities. Very few go on to school, travel, or even read anything except newspapers, to say nothing of developing artistic or musical skills. Somewhere between the hard-driving of Western capitalism, where the means becomes the end, and the laid-back, easy going style of Greek village life, there exists a third alternative. Indeed it is this creative mix of work, recreation and artistic and intellectual growth that we are seeking, both for our selves and for our students, by coming to Crete.

Our explorations of the various cultural contours of Sitia also led us to investigate some of the many villages in the mountains directly above the town itself. It so happened that the only bus up to these villages came directly past our villa, but did so at 6 A.M. The driver almost refused to stop for us, so convinced was he that we did not know where we were going. After passing Russa Eklesia, the village directly above our villa, the road turned to dirt and began winding its way through several tiny, semi-deserted villages. Finally it reached a very rocky plateau at the top of the mountain, leading directly toward a larger, more prosperous looking village. About 50 homes, all nestled together on a small hillside were surrounded with farm land and grape arbors. The sign said "Sitanos" and we decided to get off the bus.

Quite a number of folks were making their way to the church, but otherwise the place was altogether quiet, simply bathing in the early morning sunshine. As we strolled through the few tiny streets and lanes, we surmised that today was a special church holy day for this village. Like other remote villages on Crete, Sitanos not only was without tourist-orientated shops, it had no stores at all. Apparently these folks did their shopping in Sitia. There was one fairly large "Kafeneeon," a sort of cultural tradition throughout Greece which serves both as a coffee bar and gathering place for the men of the village, but it was closed. We decided to explore the area around the village by foot. There were several roads leading back down or across the top of the mountain toward towns other and smaller than Sitia. Walking most of these, we encountered several wild goats, a number of sheep herds, and some spectacular views from the various hillsides.

By late morning the village was fully awake, but definitely in a holiday sort of way. Women and children ambled here and there, while the men were congregated in the Kafeneeon, dressed in suits and playing cards. The proprietor said that although they did not normally serve food, he would be happy to whip up a couple of salads and omelettes for us, if we would come back in an hour. We visited the church, which was now empty, and poked around in the small cemetery while waiting. When we came back there was a table with two chairs, all set up for lunch, smack in the center of the large room. Other than the proprietor's wife working behind the counter, Mari was the only woman in the place. So, we sat and ate our food while the 30 or so men divided their time between playing cards or backgammon and watching us. Our social discomfort was outweighed by the wholesome and delicious quality of little "banquet" and the generally friendly atmosphere of the place.

While we were there the telephone rang and the woman behind the counter answered. After the usual greetings and salutations, she turned to an amplifier and microphone set-up, announcing over an outside loudspeaker to the whole village that there was a phone call for a certain "Manolis." In a couple of minutes a young man came in and took the call. It turned out that there is but one phone in the whole village and the loudspeaker system is the way they make it useful for the entire community. A simple but direct adaptation of modern technology to rural life. After eating we walked on to the next tiny village and waited for the returning bus. While we waited a local farmer treated us to a watermelon, grapes, and figs from his garden and orchard, simply for the hospitality of it. On the bus bumping down to mountainside in the hazy afternoon, we felt privileged to have been able to share briefly in the life of these peaceful out-of-the-way places and people.

This mention of afternoon brings up another cultural characteristic common throughout Greece. Basically, morning last until noon and mid-day until about 2 P.M., while afternoon does not really begin until after siesta time and lasts until sundown. Evening begins roughly with dusk, with night-time encompassing evening and lasting until dawn. The only real difficulties arise in connection with the notions of afternoon and evening. Several times we were taken by surprise to have Yorgos and Kiki show up for the "afternoon" coffee around 6 P.M., while more than once it was necessary to be reminded that the "evening" meal to which we had been invited would begin around 9 or 10 P.M. In Greece, everything takes place later and more slowly than in the "9 to 5" Western world, which also means that "tomorrow" may well refer to sometime in the near future. There definitely seems to be a connection between this elongated approach to time and being located in close proximity to the equator.

When the students finally arrived that first September, we felt pretty well acclimated to the Sitia area and patterns so full attention could be directed to the educational program. Classes are held in the patio every weekday morning from 9 to 12 and include courses in Ancient Philosophy, Greek Culture (including an introduction to modern Greek), philosophy of Education, Greek Art, and the thought of Nikos Kazantzakis. Afternoons and evenings are free for sunbathing and swimming, socializing, and of course studying. Nearly every weekend we make a visit to an archeological site or to a nearby village such as Mochlos. The semester also includes two one-week excursions, one to the rest of Crete and Santorini, focusing on the Minoan culture, and another to Korinthos, Epidaurus, Olympia, and Delphi, exploring the classical Greek civilization. The last week of the semester is spent in Athens visiting the Akropolis and important museums, as well as traditional market places and cultural events.

On exactly the day the students arrived that first year, the Greek banks, which are nationalized, all went on strike for three weeks. This meant that the money for board and room expenses, which the college wired to us that very day, did not actually arrive until three weeks after the strike was over. It took the three extra weeks to straighten out the backlog of paper work that had accumulated during the strike. Trying to initiate an educational program by going six weeks without funds is not recommended. Fortunately, the patience and generosity of the local people, together with the students own spending money, turned what could have been a catastrophe into a mere inconvenience. Through this experience, coupled with the ensuing three-week garbage strike, the students learned that Greek people especially Cretans, take their politics very seriously and frequently engage in direct civil disobedience in order to make their preferences know.

The same can be said for Apostolis' friend Yanis Kafetzakis, who helped us find our new home at Villa Romantsa. He operates a fine art gallery and shop (Sitian Arts"), where his British wife Jane displays her lovely water colors. Yanis also plays an important role in the cultural life of Sitia. Througout the years they both have been a real source of support and friendship to us.

We began our program just at the conclusion of 8 years of socialist governance, which followed almost directly on the heels of military dictatorship of about the same duration. During the socialist regime (Pasok), under Andrea Papandreou, many public benefit programs had been instituted and a great number of bureaucratic jobs had been created. Meanwhile, the country went increasingly into debt, while living more comfortably on rolling credit. Now a much more conservative party (Nea Demokratia) was restructuring and tightening the economy, an austerity program being felt much more by the farmers and workers than by the upper class business folk. Therefore, the various unions and nationalized employees engage in sporadic strikes as a sign of their displeasure with the new government. Neither the capitalist nor the socialist governments seem to work very well in poor countries like Greece, where the money necessary for the programs of the latter is not available and what money there is largely in the hands of the leaders of the former.

During the weeks of waiting for the college money to arrive, the people at the bank became and have remained good friends. They were nearly as frustrated as we about the seeming "disappearance" of our funds, and there was a constant stream of telexes, phone calls, and wiring back and forth between Sitia, Athens and New York. It got so that twice a day I would merely stop at the open door of the bank, catch the manager's eye and twist my uplifted hand in the manner that always signals a question in Greece. He, in turn, would simply tip his head back and roll his eyes slightly to signify a negative answer to my question. The nearly rigid regularity with which these various hand and facial gestures accompany verbal communication is a salient feature of the Greek language. One can often "overhear" a conversation taking place clear across the plaza, simply by paying attention to the gestures. This aspect of spoken Greek is far more specific and characteristic in its patterns than the merely "talking with your hands" phenomenon generally associated with the linguistic patterns of other Mediterranean peoples.

The students always find our excursions extremely interesting and enjoyable, especially those to Mochlos and Santorini. On Santorini we usually stay at a family run hotel on the south rim and near the Akrotiri excavation. Tasoula, along with her husband, children, and in-laws, always goes out of her way to make sure everything is to our liking. The combination of excellent food, a private beach, along with the ever-present beauty that is Santorini, render this out of the way location especially charming. Also, this past year a trip to a Cretan mountain village named Axos was added to our itinerary. Although the nightly program, presented by local young people, is designed strictly for tourists, the evening program of authentic Cretan dance performance and participation, together with ample wine and scrumptious food, makes for lively enjoyment and a lasting memory. The young dancers are truly gifted and fascinating, and there is one 80 year old Palikari who dances with nearly all the young tourist women while wiggling his eyebrows and stealing kisses.

Another visit that has recently been added to the program takes us to the centuries old monasteries of Meteora in central Greece. Coming as it does at the conclusion of our tour of classical Greek sites, this trip serves as an excellent transition to our study of medieval Greece and the Orthodox church. The sight of these monasteries, perched atop the huge meteor-like boulders, which give the place its name, is literally breathtaking. In addition, going up the mountain road and into the monasteries themselves carries one into a different time and place, one seemingly completely separate from the world below. Until recent decades the only way up to the monasteries was by rope hoisted basket. The day of our visit the weather was quite foggy, with the shrouding of the rock bound monasteries floating in space adding immensely to the mystery of it all. In the little shops operated by each monastery, students bought copies of ancient relics and icons, as well as cassette tapes of monks engaged in chanting rituals.

Back in Sitia the students attend at least one Orthodox church service as part of the course in Greek culture. Since most of them are Roman Catholic, the highly liturgical nature of the service is somewhat familiar, but the fact that the priest speaks in biblical Greek and keeps disappearing within the alter leaves them pretty confused. The two hours of standing and the general separation of men in the back from women in the front also trouble them a bit. After having read and discussed a pretty thorough book on the history, beliefs, and practices of Orthodoxy, we visit a local church for a brief lecture about the service and a question period. The students are always a bit surprised, but largely pleased to discover that Orthodox priests can and generally do marry. At every such session there is inevitably one student who asks if the church will ever ordain women. The total rejection of this idea is always as clearly expressed through the priest's body language as it is through the interpreter's verbal translation of the negative answer.

In contrast to nearly every other branch of Christendom, the Orthodox church stands in direct opposition to nearly all efforts to establish dialogue and/or union within world Christianity. Essentially the only concessions the church has made to modern developments is to recommend that services in non-Greek or Russian speaking countries be conducted in two languages, the traditional one and the local one, and to allow chairs or pews for the congregation to sit in. In Greece the priests have commonly become relatively wealthy, as has the church as a whole, mostly through land ownership. This, together with the inflexible attitude toward any change practice and style, has slowly but surely served to alienate recent generations from Orthodoxy. Although the church is everywhere present within Greek culture and custom, only the older generation actually practices it.

My young friend Manolis, whom I met playing basketball, is planning to be a priest, but first he must get married and study theology. Initially he had planned to be a teacher of religion at the high school level, but he decided against it because, in his own words: "I do not want to spend my life trying to teach about religious beliefs and practices to young people who are not at all interested in them." When I suggested that his interest and considerable talent in basketball might help him establish a point of contact with such young people, he replied: "Oh, I will have to give up playing basketball when I let my beard grow and wear a long, black robe." A local priest confirmed Manolis opinion when I asked him if this would really be necessary. "When the boy becomes a priest, he will have more important things to do than play basketball," was the answer. This attitude is, unfortunately, highly reflective of the church's traditionalism, and may well prove to be the main cause of its continuing diminishing influence among the people of Greece.

Returning to Sitia after these excursions to other parts of Greece is a genuinely exciting experience for the students. Not only do they find themselves looking forward to being back among familiar surroundings and friendly faces, but the people of Sitia are honestly pleased to see them. By November, when all of the tourists have left town, the students have made a number of friends and it feels good to be with them again. Many of these friends are invited to our Thanksgiving dinner celebration at a local restaurant where, Pam, the English cook, knows how to prepare turkey "with all the trimin's." The dinner is even preceded by a rag-tag, rather hilarious football game on the beach.

There are two other aspects of our efforts to enculturate the students into Greek society that are worthy of mention before bringing this chapter to a close. One is the Wednesday evening meal when we gather together to share our fledgling efforts at cooking various Greek food. Each week each apartment prepares a different dish or part of the meal, and while courageously and politely sampling the results of these experiments, we swap stories about our recent cross-cultural experiences and/or embarrassments. After dinner our friend Katerina, the local physical education and dance teacher, gives her weekly lesson in Cretan folk dancing. She is a vibrant, humorous middle-aged woman who simply loves to teach dancing, and since she knows very little English her instructions and counting out of the steps in Greek serve as an excellent supplement to our study of the language. Katarina's group of young folk dancers performs regularly in Sitia and also makes occasional tours to various cities throughout Greece.

The next year, through the generosity of our good friend and "angel" Bill, we engaged a young Greek school teacher to instruct our students in Greek. Toula teaches English in one of the nearby highschools, and in addition to her "official" duties as our Greek teacher, she became a real friend of ours and of our students. Toula even arranged to have several of our students, who were education majors back home, visit her classes at the Greek highschool. We are all extremely grateful for Toula's participation in our program.

Not the least of the dividends of our new home in Sitia is its close proximity to Mochlos. In addition to our regularly scheduled weekend visit there, which several students always choose to repeat on their own, we ourselves are able to meander back every now and then. Moreover, many of the folks in Mochlos frequently visit Sitia to shop or visit friends and relatives. Young Anna, the daughter of a Mochlos couple we know, comes every weekday to attend high school. Thus we actually see many of our friends on the street on an almost daily basis. In this way the two places which have come to mean so much to us are woven together in our daily lives as they are in our memories.

In the previous chapters the emphasis was on specific places and people of Crete, together with my experience and memories of them. In the following chapters I will focus on more historical and philosophical dimensions of Crete, along with my own reflections there on. The specific content of these chapters will be the ancient Minoan culture, the classical Greek heritage, and the thought of Nikos Kazantzakis. Together these three themes form the broader loom on which my own encounter with Crete has been woven.

In 1900 a wealthy British gentleman named Arthur Evans, one of the early practitioners of the then young science of archaeology, began digging in a large hillside, known as Knossos, a few miles south of Iraklion. In a very short time it became evident that Evans had discovered the palatial center of an ancient and highly refined civilization. In fact, there are a number of good reasons for thinking that this complex and widespread culture was the historical basis for the ancient Greek stories of King Minos, Theseus and Ariadne, Daedalus and Icarus, Minotaurs and Labyrinths, and the like. The story of this discovery, against the back drop of its historical and archaeological significance, is told in an extremely interesting way by Leonard Cottrell in his book, The Bull of Minos. He quotes Evans' own estimate of his findings: "We know that the old traditions were true. We have before our eyes a wondrous spectacle-the resurgence, namely, of a civilization twice as old as that of Hellas. It is true that on the old Palace site what we see are only the ruins of ruins, but the whole is still inspired with Minos's spirit of order and organization, and the free and natural art of the great architect Daedalus. The spectacle indeed, that we have here before us is assuredly of world-wide significance" (page 179). In the following summary of the details and contours of this fascinating ancient culture I shall be relying on Stylianos Alexiou's excellent Minoan Civilization.

The main phases of Minoan history can be divided into four periods. The first from 2600-2000 B.C., is called the "pre-palatial" because during this time the Minoans worked with copper and bronze, but had not yet constructed any palace-like stone buildings. Between 2000 and 1700 B.C. the first palace was built at Knossos,

Knossos Palace

and this is termed the "proto-palatial" period. Around 1700 B.C. this first palace was destroyed by gigantic earthquakes and fire. New and finer palatial structures were erected right on top of these ruins, so the period from 1700 to 1450 is referred to as the "Neo-palatial" period. Sometime around 1450 B.C. the volcanic island of Thera (now Santorini) erupted, producing a violent catastrophe that partially destroyed and greatly weakened the entire island civilization, allowing Mycenaeans from mainland Greece to conquer and occupy it. This "post-palatial" period lasted from 1450 to about 1100 B.C., when it was destroyed by the Dorian invaders from Northern Europe.

One catches something of the historical and cultural significance of this chronology when it is understood that the Minoan civilization not only endured but thrived for over a thousand years and was on its way out nearly a thousand years before the rise of what we know as the Golden Age of Classical Greece. This significance is further enhanced by a consideration of the amazing cultural achievements of this ancient island civilization.

These achievements pertain especially to the areas of technology, trade, and aesthetic sensitivity. It is also important to know that the Minoans not only inhabited Crete in large numbers, having built at least six other smaller palaces near the coastline on the eastern half of the island, but that they also established towns and outposts on the Cycladic islands, such as Santorini. As was mentioned in Chapter One, even the village of Mochlos is turning out to have been an important late Minoan center.

With the introduction of bronze by peoples migrating to the Cyclades and Crete from what is now Turkey, around 2600 B.C., the technological development of the Minoans escalated extremely rapidly. In addition to a huge increase in metal objects, both practical and ornamental, the potters wheel and kiln became well known at this stage. Near the year 2000, when great advancements were made in ceramic quality and variety, the Minoans also orchestrated the erection of vast and complex structures and Knossos, Phaestos, Mallia, and Kato Zakros. In addition to requiring a great deal of architectural vision and engineering knowledge, such projects surely required a large degree of political power and organization. Although these palaces were nearly completely destroyed in the earthquakes of 1700 B.C., the Minoans rebuilt them in for greater magnificence very shortly. Alexiou speculates about the political significance of such palatial rule: "Peace and prosperity, the so-called Pax Minoica reigned in Crete, shown by the complete absence of fortifications. It seems likely that the ruler of Knossos was recognized as overlord everywhere in the island. One theory holds that the Cretan palaces do not represent the seats of different kings and princes, but that all belonged to one ruler, that of Knossos, who after the pattern of Oriental monarchs, had palaces in every town, which he visited in turn" (page 30).

The New Palaces featured majestic alabaster staircases and entry-ways, flanked by colonnades of brightly painted cedar

Knossos Cedar Columns

columns, large limestone courtyards, with many lightwells and porches which could be closed off by folding wooden doors during the cooler winter monts. Throughout the palaces there were life sized wall paintings and frescoes depicting Minoan palace life and naturalistic scenes of Cretan land and sea, plant and animal life. In addition, the Minoan palaces included a very complex water

Knossos Lightwells

system, made of fitted terra cota pipes, for carrying fresh water to and waste water from every part of the main lower floors, The queen's chamber even had water running through its toilet, a kind of flushing toilet.

In design and execution these palaces were truly marvelous. The story has it that when the first rains came after Arthur Evans had uncovered the ruins of Knossos, the drainage system worked perfectly, even after nearly four thousand years! The design and colors of the brightly painted murals were also nearly perfectly preserved by the dry, hot soil of Crete, and they are now kept behind glass in the Iraklion Museum. Evans undertook to partially restore and reconstruct various walls and rooms at Knossos, so as to enable the visitor to get a feel for the structure and ambiance of the palaces. Although contemporary and more scientific minded archaeologists are embarrawed by such procedures, any non-specialist who has visited the essentially flat ruins of the more recently excavated palaces will be grateful for Evan's imaginative efforts.

Of course the Minoans did not all live in the palaces, but in the many towns and villages surrounding them and scattered throughout Crete and other Mediterranean islands. Moreover, the Minoan trading ships travelled frequently to Syria, Turkey, and Egypt. In fact, pictures of young Minoan men bearing gifts appeared on the walls of Egyptian tombs. The excavation near Akrotiri on Santorini is especially revealing of the wide circumfrance and elaborate development of Minoan culture. The town currently being uncovered there, with its many streets, stairways, two and three-storied buildings, and bright, highly animated frescoes, seems quite complex and self-sufficient even without a palace. After the terrible eruption of Santorini, which clearly seems to have precipitated a gigantic tidal wave that inundated the entire north coast of Crete, the Minoan palaces and culture were gradually taken over by peoples from the mainland, thereby forming the basis for the transition to the rise and dominance of the Mycenaean culture. Some three hundred years later the Dorian invaders brought an end to the vestiges of the Minoan civilization and to Crete's historical importance in ancient times.

Knossos Inney Chamber

In addition to the excavated pa-laces, towns, and villas, the thousands of fascinating artifacts tell us a great deal about the Minoan way of life. The beautiful frescoes, painted with pigments of mineral origin or derived from metallic oxides, are replete with bright reds, yellows, blues and reveal courtly activity and dress. Also, many miniature frescoes which portray individual persons or nature scenes, have been found throughout Crete; they seem to have been strictly for ornamentation. Thousands of small sculptures have been found, the most common and well-known are representations of royalty, goddesses, and animals, especially bulls. Most of these appear to be molded out of a mixture of sand and clay, bound together by resin and colored with a metallic oxide mixed with alkali, giving them a blue-green, glazed surface. Some statuettes made of ivory have been discovered, as well as many beautiful stone vases used for oil libations and other religious rituals.

Many of these artifacts display royal fashions, such as the open bodice of the Snake Goddess, while others seem to honor specific animals, such as the bull, the dolphin, and the snake. All human bodies, as with animal and plant life, are depicted in graceful postures and loose-fitting, flowing clothes. The acrobats portrayed in the midst of the daring "bull games," which seems to have been a common and highly significant event in palace life, are

Minoan Acrobats

scantily clad and differentiated by skin-color, white for the women and red for the men. Nearly everyone's hair is long, curly, and flowing in the wind. The women clearly paid a great deal of attention to make-up, jewelry and stylish dress. Although there is some similarity to the Egyptian practice of presenting the front-view of the body and eye along with a side-view of the face, the Minoan artists portrayed the human body far more gracefully and sensuously than did those of Egypt.

Minoan Jags

Minoan pottery evolved rapidly from simple hand built bowls and jugs to large, elongated vases and storage jars thrown on a wheel. The early color scheme was black with white and red trim, generally designated "Kam†res style," with the lines mainly following wavy or spiral patterns. Often the vases were decorated with representations of flowers and sea life, especially fish and octopi. Many of these same designs are found on the many thousands of "seal stones" which the Minoans seemed to have used for personal identification and even, perhaps, various games. Bronze was used for huge cauldrons and many tools of different kinds. A large number of the famous "Double Axes," a symbol found everywhere in Minoan ruins, have been collected and can be seen, along with most of these other artifacts, in the Iraklion Museum. There are also many fine Minoan artifacts in the museums of Sitia and Agios Nikolaos.

A person experiences a deep sense of wonder when confronted by the remains of such an ancient and splendid civilization. Standing in a museum, imagining an actual person working away on a stone vase or clay pot with these particular implements, or wearing the jewelry and garments depleted in the frescoes, is both an exhilarating and a humbling experience. Walking through the excavated ruins of the Minoan palaces, actually stepping on the very same stones as those people did four thousand years ago, is truly awe-inspiring. Even sitting on a hillside, gazing across the mountainous Cretan landscape at the Mediterranean Sea, you can almost feel the presence of those ancient folks, sitting in the same spot watching the trade ships return from a voyage to Egypt. Such experiences fill one with a genuine sense of mystery concerning time, human nature, and the meaning of life. The Minoans also confront us with two far more specific, yet equally intriguing mysteries.

The first such mystery revolves around the translation of Minoan writing. All of the interpretations of this civilization offered by historians and archaeologists are inferred from the excavated palaces and artifacts, together with a dose of ancient Greek mythology. For, despite their amazing artistic interests and abilities, the Minoans seem not to have been at all literary. At least as of yet nothing resembling scrolls or inscriptions have been found which would tell us what these people believed, how they lived, and so on. All that have been found are a few small tablets and fragments which seem to be lists of products or bills of sale, but even these, written in what scholars call "Linear A," have not been translated. No one has yet been able to decipher the symbol system in which they are written.

A different symbol system, designated "Linear B," has also been found, but once again only in bits and pieces which seem to have been part of lists of products or trade items. In addition, a good number of fragments have been collected, presumably from early Minoan times, on which are inscribed a wide variety of "ideograms" or picture-symbols, somewhat similar to Egyptian hieroglyphic writing but no direct linguistic connection has been established. These "pictographs" often depict recognizable household or natural objects, but since there are well over one hundred different signs, there seems to be no way they could have functioned phonetically. At the Phaestos palace Arthur Evans also discovered a clay disk on both sides of which are carved a good number of such symbols, arranged in a spiral pattern progressing out from the center.

This "Phaestos Disk," which is about seven inches in diameter and is on display in the Iraklion museum, contains many easily recognizable pictures of people, birds, plants, and the like, each separated by vertical lines within the spiral pattern. Unfortunately, this artifact is unique, and as yet no one has been able to offer a convincing theory concerning its origin and use, let alone its conceptual meaning. Because of its unique character and characters, many scholars believe either that the disk had an important ritualistic significance, or that it is not Minoan in origin. Perhaps with all the continued excavations at many fresh Minoan sites, some light will be cast on the nature of this interesting but puzzling disk. As Professor Chadwick explains in his book, Reading the Past: "If we had an adequate sample, such problems might be resolved, but we cannot even identify the type to which the language belongs, much less its linguistic family. We do not know the place of origin of the script, and as shown above there is a fair chance that it is not native to Crete, though this cannot be excluded. We have no means of guessing, even approximately, the nature of the text, for nothing like it has been found written in any know language. All this could change if more specimens of the script were to be found. No script is in theory undecipherable, even if the language is totally unknown. But in order to make any progress it is essential to have enough texts, and these must be sufficiently variable, not merely repetitious of the same few formulas. Moreover, some of the inscriptions must be found in contexts which allow us to deduce approximately the meaning of some words without reference to their phonetic values. Only a large deposit of similar documents could open the way to a true decipherment of the Phaistos Disk" (page 60).

What is really needed in order to clear up the mystery of Minoan writing is the discovery of a library or hidden collection of sacred writings, such as have been found at Qumran in Palestine and at Naghamadi in Egypt. Also of great help would be some sort of bilingual record, similar to the "Rosetta Stone," in which the same material is inscribed twice, first in Linear A and again in some already deciphered language. However, given the amount of digging that has already taken place, with extremely negligible results, it hardly seems likely that such discoveries will be forthcoming. It appears that the Minoans lacked the ability or the desire, which generally go hand-in-hand, to develop a written language with which to carry on their business and record their important events. Given their highly developed aesthetic sensitivity, this absence of a literary heritage is surely a puzzling phenomenon, however.

One possible interpretation of the lack of writing in the Minoan culture is the reverse of the situation obtaining with respect to Jewish and Muslim culture. In these latter two cases there exists of religious prohibition of visual representation in general and of deity in particular. Thus written language, in the form of story, history, and poetry, plays and highly significant role in both of these cultures. Contrariwise, it is possible that the Minoans had some sort of religious scruples against the written word, or at least reserving it for sacred and secret use. As with the Jewish taboo against writing the name of Jehovah, perhaps the Minoans were in such awe of the power of language that they regulated or suppressed its public use. Assuredly, this is only an hypothesis, but the absence of written language in a culture so highly developed seems to require something of a special explanation.

Toward the end of the Minoan era, around 1500 B.C., the already mentioned "Linear B" came into use, both on Crete and on Cyprus. The peoples from the mainland, usually called Achaeans or Mycenaeans, who took possession of Minoan palaces and towns after the catastrophe of 1470, made use of this new script in transcribing the various prosperities and accomplishments of their royalty. Having heard Arthur Evans lecture in Oxford about the mystery surrounding the ancient tablets bearing these cryptic symbol systems, the then young Michael Ventris dedicated some twenty years of his life to the decipherment of Linear B. With help from Professor John Chadwick, he was able to demonstrate that this script was actually a primitive form of ancient Greek and was used by the peoples of Asia Minor (now Turkey) as well. Professor Chadwick's Reading the Past gives an excellent account of this scholarly adventure. The fact remains, however, that not only does Linear A remain undeciphered, but the content

Knossos Royal Theater

of the fragments involved tell us next to nothing about Minoan culture, its beliefs, practices, and history.

The other major mystery surrounding the phenomenon of Minoan culture concerns the circumstances of its collapse as a major factor in the Mediterranean world. On the one hand, it is clear that catastrophic earthquakes and tidal waves, emanating from Santorini around 1470, played an important and dramatic role in the demise of this civilization, as did invasions from mainland peoples. Although the Mycenaeans adopted and adapted many aspects of Minean culture into their own, much as the Romans were to do for the Greeks centuries later, it is not difficult to tell the difference between the two cultures in either case. At their best the later societies represent a fair imitation of the artistic ability and sensitivity of the original, while at their worst they clearly reveal a far more power-oriented, pedestrian way of life. The genius of the Minoans, like that of the Greeks after them, was partially extended but inevitably lost by those who came immediately after them.

On the other hand, there is an increasing number of scholars who are in agreement with the idea that the Minoan civilization, and especially its sudden collapse and disappearance, is the historical basis for the ancient legend of lost Atlantis. Plato recounts the story which Solon heard in Egypt about the highly advanced island civilization located in the Atlantic Ocean, just outside the strait of Gibralter, which sank suddenly in a great catastrophe. Even though the description of the layout of the legendary Atlantis, which does not particularly fit that of Crete or Santorini, and the location outside the Mediterranean Sea are factors that militate against such an interpretive possibility, there are a number of factors that would seem to support it. In his fascinating book, The End of Atlantis, Professor J. V. Luce provides a thorough examination of the evidence relevant to a consideration of this issue.

The advanced character of the seafaring Minoan culture, together with its rather sudden demise in the wake of the explosion of Thera, surely support at least a remarkable parallel between the Atlantis legend and the Minoan reality. It is clear that the Minoans had well-established trade relations with Egypt and the sudden termination of these would give rise to stories and speculations as to the cause thereof. Moreover, the fact that the Minoan civilization essentially came to an end nearly a thousand years before Solon visited Egypt would account for the discrepancies between the two stories. More specifically, the actual destruction of Thera, as a result of the gigantic volcanic eruption, literally resulted in the sudden sinking of a large and important Minoan center. The extremely large excavation at Santorini testifies to the probable magnitude of this extension of the Cretan culture, since it is more than likely that there were other Minoan towns, cities, and even palaces on Therea as well as on there Cycladic islands.

The geological evidence pertaining to the eruption of Thera has even led some thinkers to speculate about the connection between it and the departure of the Hebrew people from Egypt, as recorded in the book of Exodus. The volcanic ash from this eruption, carried by the prevailing northwest winds, has been found over a widespread area to the southeast of Thera, covering the eastern half of Crete, all of Egypt, and part of Palestine. Based on seismographic data concerning the almost unbelievable force and fallout associated with this eruption, it can be assumed that the ensuing shock waves caused great destruction for hundreds of miles around and that the ash-filled sky completely blocked out the sun for a number of days. It has been suggested by some that such factors might well cause the widespread disruption a natural patterns and cycles, as well as the social panic, described in the book of Exodus.

The chief difficulty with this theory is that the date of the explosion of Thera, certainly between 1500 and 1450 B.C., is at least three hundred years too early to coincide with the best evidence surrounding the Hebrew's departure from Egypt. Nevertheless, there are scholars who question these dates. One such thinker, whose works continue to be the center of serious controversy, is Immanuel Velikovsky. In his book Worlds in Collision Velikovsky tried to take seriously the nearly universal myths of floods, earthquakes, and planetary disruptions in defending the possibility that in not-too-distant prehistoric times Venus intersected the earth's atmosphere, causing violent and widespread natural upheaval. Although his proposal was roundly denigrated by the vast majority of astrophysicists, an increasing number of Velikovsky's predictions, based on his hypothesis, are being confirmed. The most dramatic of these confirmations was the incredibly hot temperature of Venus, which scientists had agreed was cold, revealed by recent Explorer satellite missions in solar space.

In his more recent book, Ages in Chaos, Velikovsky comes to the conclusion that there exists a four hundred year discrepancy between the historical accounts of their times offered by the ancient Egyptians and those offered by the Hebrews. Although it remains unclear whose calendar of events contains the error, as well as what motive might account for it, it seems impossible to correlate these two records as we now have them. If this difficulty could be overcome, it might prove possible to integrate the eruption of Thera with the departure of the Hebrews from Egypt. This might also cast light on a possible connection between the end of the Minoan civilization and the Egyptian story of lost Atlantis. Until some of these puzzles can be solved, however, the full story of the fading away of the Minoans will continue to remain a mystery.

Over the years I have spent a good many hours reflecting on the significance of various dimensions of this ancient Cretan civilization known as the Minoans. One of the important aspects of this culture which has captured my attention is its aesthetic sensibility. To begin with the obvious, there is a strong naturalistic character in nearly everything the Minoans crafted. Unlike other ancient societies, the Minoans made the natural world of plants, animals, birds, and fish the main subject matter of their art. Although representations of human beings is also a main Minoan artistic motif, it is plant and animal life that dominate the frescoes, pottery, statuary, and jewelry. Even the palatial architecture, though always rectangular in shape, is adapted to the rolling quality of the Cretan landscape, fitted to the step-like arrangement of the hillside. This architectural adaptation even went so far as to develop ways of bringing light and fresh air inside the palace structure by means of wide and deep stairwells, together with folding and multiple windows. Professor R. Higgins describes the practical advantages of this type of architecture in his book <u>Minoan and Mycenaean Art</u>:

> By means of light-wells (that is to say, small courtyards) it was possible to extend in any direction without sacrificing light or ventilation, and this was done." There is little obvious sense of planning in a Cretan palace, much of gradual and organic growth. It was no doubt this maze-like effect, still to be observed gave rise to the legend of Theseus and the Labyrinth. Another feature which facilitated this kind of expansion was the use of flat roofs, which make casual extensions a much easier business than when gables are used (pp.22-23).

In addition to the content of Minoan art being naturalistic in character, there is as well a natural grace to its quality, a flow of line and shape which suggests those of the natural world. In fact, on occasion this preference for curving and undulating lines and shapes, which stands in complete contrast to the Egyptian aesthetic sensibility, causes the Minoan artists to falsify the actual physical characteristics of the natural object being represented. Frequently, certain features of the various species of natural life seem to be deliberately elongated and rounded in order to emphasize their elasticity and movement. The different parts of the human body, for instance, in both paintings and sculptures, are hardly ever represented as distinct, functioning units, but are depicted as flowing out of and into one another by means of continuous lines.

Speaking of the various aspects of aesthetic naturalistim in this way suggests a schematic which may prove helpful in understanding the overall character of Minoan art, or that of any other culture for that matter. On the one hand, it is possible to speak of an artistic spectrum running between form and function, while on the other hand, one can posit an interesting continuum between representation and expression. This schematic, which facilitates a multi-dimensional correlation of these four crucial aspects of aesthetic activity, would look like this:

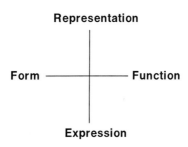

Returning to our consideration of Minoan architecture, it is possible to recognize the dynamics of the first of these continual at work in the palatial structures on Crete. Not unlike the creations of Frank Lloyd Wright, the Minoan palaces are a remarkable blend of form and function. Not only are they built along the lines of the hillside terrain, but their roofs, porches, and stairwells facilitate access to the various levels as well as providing protection while making a maximum amount of sunlight and fresh air. In addition, these multi-leveled, rectangular structures also facilitated further additions and connections to and among the various levels and venues. Moreover, since the palaces served as both the private living quarters for the royalty and public ceremonial space, the layered and staggered architecture offered maximum privacy and free access simultaneously.

This integration of form and function can also be seen in the various large frescoes and murals found throughout the Minoan palaces and villas. Such paintings serve not only to depict and reinforce the royal way of life, but to decorate and inspire as well. In this connection, one cannot help being struck by the almost complete absence of the sort of "royalty-worship" scenes which seem to characterize the visual arts of other ancient civilizations. Animal, plant, and sealife dominate Minoan paintings, rather than Kings, Queens, and warriors. In fact, the total lack of emphasis on battles and fortifications throughout the Minoan culture is a subject to which we shall return shortly. For now it is sufficient to note that the tone set by Minoan architecture is one of peaceful grandeur, and there is every reason to believe that the people themselves valued and embodied these characteristics, as well.

The same pattern of "form serving function" in incorporated into Minoan statuary and pottery. While there seem to have been almost no large public statues, there was an abundance of small figurines used for jewelry, worship, and games. Often as not the shape of these statuettes is formed so as to facilitate handling. In like manner, the various forms of pottery, whether practical or ritualistic, like that of nearly all peoples, are shaped in accord with their domestic or ceremonial purpose. Nevertheless, contrary to a great number of ancient and modern plastic or ceramic artifacts, the Minoans almost never found it necessary to sacrifice, or even ignore, the aesthetic form in deference to the practical function. The graceful lines and dynamic proportions characteristic of the Minoan aesthetic can be encountered in nearly every piece of art created by Cretan artisans.

At the same time, the relationship between content and expression in Minoan art can be seen to be equally symbiotic. Although there are a number of nonrepresentational patterns within Minoan visual and plastic arts, the vast majority of designs involve the representation of aspects of the natural or human world. An abundant variety of plant, animal, and sea life, as well as various aspects of palace life, are portrayed in nearly all Minoan creations. In no way, however, can these depictions be interpreted as mere representation. For once again, the warmth and vibrancy of the way Minoan people experienced and interacted with their environment clearly expresses itself with uncommon, yet characteristic force in everything they created. Both the active and latent movement of the birds, the octopi, and even the people, is conveyed and directly by means of the simple, curved lines and shapes in the rendering of natural objects. Minoan artists seem to have found a happy balance between the meaningful representation of nature and various modes of self-expression.

Nowhere is this blending of content and expression more clearly evident than in the famous fresco of the young acrobats performing on the charging bull. Although the figures of both the bull and the young acrobats are readily recognizable for what they represent, considerable effort has been expended to portray them as dynamically and gracefully active. Furthermore, a certain formal quality pervades the painting, as if to convey the ritualistic character of the event. In addition, the arms and legs of the acrobats are considerably elongated, and they are colored differently so as to differentiate the men from the women. Thus representation can be adapted to fit expression in the same way as form can be integrated into function. Professor Higgins summarizes the Minoan aesthetic clearly, if a bit too briefly: "The style is the first truly naturalistic style to be found in European, or indeed in any art. It includes the two chief Cretan characteristics: the reproduction of natural forms in a vivid and impressionistic manner, and the ability to fit the painting to the area to be decorated" (p. 95).

A second feature of the Minoan culture on which I have reflected repeatedly is their religious life. Although our lack of written materials greatly limits the depth and range of inquiry into this topic, a few highly suggestive explorations may be ventured on the basis of the extent artifacts. Professor Alexiou introduces the subject in the following way: "It seems that the 'vegetation cycle,' a feature of primitive cults, was fundamental to the religion of the Minoans" (p. 70). More broadly put, all ancient peoples were as much in awe of the birth, growth and death cycle, whether in relation to plant and animal life or human life as they were dependent on it. Both this awe and dependence gave rise to the elemental forms of religious life, namely fear and honor. The early Minoans, like other Neo-lithic peoples, seems to have centered their religious concerns and practices around the process of regeneration as embodied in the annual Spring time renewal of vegetation and the birth-giving female body. Both of these phenomena must have been as mysterious as they were powerful to pre-historic cultures.

It is often maintained by scholars in this field that ancient peoples "invented" religion in order to manipulate these mysterious powers of reproduction in their own favor, in order to "bargain" with gods and demons. Thus the rituals and taboos of ancient religions, such as raindances, animal or human sacrifices, and cave paintings, are generally interpreted as efforts to appease or please otherwise hostile supernatural forces. My own studies and reflections on these matters, however, make it seem more likely that ancient worshippers were attempting to "participate" in the regenerative processes and cycles by means of their rituals and taboos, rather than bargaining with whatever controlled them. I myself think this "marketing" interpretation is far too dependent on modernist assumptions about the "primitive mentality" of "savage" peoples. It should be remembered, for instance, that Native Americans did not perform rain dances and buffalo rituals whenever they wanted rain and buffalo. Rather, they did so when it was appropriate in relation to the planting and hunting cycles.

From this vantage point, it is possible and more helpful to think of ancient religion, including Minoan, as an effort to join in with the processes and cycles which govern regeneration, rather than an attempt at adversarial manipulation. The world operates, after all, according to certain principles and wise people learn to understand them and align themselves with them, for purposes of both survival and well-being. Just as one is careful around high cliffs and seeks to eat nutritional food, so one pays attention to and participates in regenerative processes so as to facilitate a life which is in harmony with the natural patterns of existence. Mystery and awe do not only produce fear and defensiveness; they can also yield joy and gratitude, depending on the way and degree to which one interacts with them.

Thus the symbols and corresponding rituals of the early Minoans, which apparently revolved around fertility cycles, may be viewed as a complex means of participating in and contributing to the powerful forces which make life possible. The paintings of freshly blooming plant life, figurines of pregnant women and young mothers holding their child, together with the rituals associated with them, can be understood as ways of celebrating and reinforcing the natural fertility cycles. There can be little doubt that the earth, out of which sprang and grew all vegetation, if not birds and fish as well, was conceived of as both female and divine by the Minoans. Also, because they participated in this regeneration process in a special way through childbirth, women seem to have been viewed as in some divine sense. There are myriads of fragments and seal stones bearing images of female goddesses and/or rulers, and nearly as many statuettes of the "Snake Goddess" in a variety of forms.

There are at least five important features of these "Snake Goddesses" that bear special mentioning. The first is the elaborate, most probably royal dress and hat or crown, as the case may be. The second is the forcefully erect, obviously authoritative posture of these statuettes, with arms extended as if performing some official function or ritual. Thirdly, the bodice of these figures is invariably designed as open, exposing full breasts, as if to suggest fecundency and nurture. Fourthly, generally these women are holding in their hands snakes, a symbol of power within the earth. Lastly, perched on top of the Goddess' hat or crown there is often an owl, the symbol of celestial wisdom. It should be noted, in addition, that a good number of these small statues and finurines are made of ivory and gold painted with bright colors, suggesting refinement and expense.

Without launching into a diatribe on the cosmic significance of or even a preference for, female deity, it must be achnowledged that the history of Western religions betrays a decided one-sidedness in favor of patriarchial religions. It must be admitted, as well, that a great deal that is of value was lost when the motherly, nurturing character of divine reality was forced into the background by this overemphsis of male divinity. Moreover, it is arguable that the irresponsible attitude of Western culture toward its environments tems directly from the suppression of any divine dimension within the notion of "Mother Nature." To be sure, the dominance of scientific objectivity and experimentation have also contributed strongly to our tendency to view natural processes as impersonal and essentially mundane. The movement toward ecological awareness and responsibility has viewed the possibility of viewing these processes as both divine and female in character, albeit in a reciprocal fashion.

All the evidence points to the fact that the Minoans fully understood and celebrated the regenerative and nurturing power of nature and its cyclical patterns, and to them it seemed appropriate to incorporate and express this in their religion in the form of a female deity. In this connection it is important to add that the Minoans also seem to have worshipped a young male God, a tamer of wild beasts, who each year entered into sacred marriage with the Earth Goddess, died, and was resurrected again the next spring. At the same time, there appears to have been a certain degree of worship surrounding a Bull God, who symbolized both male potency and the power of the earth, especially in connection with earthquakes. Many of these beliefs and practices found their way into classical Greek Mythology and religion, such as in the stories of the birth of Zeus, the Minotaur, and Athena the Goddess of Justice and Victory.

Although we are greatly limited by the absence of a body of Minoan literature from which to derive a thorough and precise knowledge of the religion of these ancient Cretans, it seems fair to surmise that it involved a good deal of animal sacrifice and ceremonies concerning the dead. Many of the pictographic fragments depict such rituals and a large number of what appear to be lustral basins and libation jugs have been found. In addition, very many grave sites and tombs have been excavated, especially in mountain caves, where a gret deal of attention seems to have been given to specific procedures. The places of worship also seem to have been caves and mountain tops, although special small buildings and public courtyards appear to have been used as well. There is at least one instance, ner the village of Archanes, where the sacrifice of a young prince by an older priest seems to have been interrupted by an extremely violent earthquake (National Geographic, Feb. 1981).

For myself, I am both enlightened and comforted, as well as challenged, by the naturalistic and female qualities of ancient Cretan religion. As with the Native American and African tribal religions I have had opportunity to study, Minoan religion achieved a dynamic balance of the divine and the natural, including human existence. It did this primarily through an emphasis on cyclical regeneration and fertility, as mediated in plant and animal life, and especially in female reproduction and nature. Professor Nanno Marinatos, in her book Art and Religion in Thera, succinctly summarizes most of the points mentioned in the foregoing pages thusly: "In conlusion, nature scenes in Minoan art are more symbolic than naturalistic." "They allude to the general comcept of fertility and fecundity in the spring. Very often they provide a setting for the appearance of the Minoan goddess and for ritual action;at other times they are just the background for cult activities which take place in the room in which they were painted" (p.96).

One other important dimension of the Minoan civilizatin upon which I have reflected a good deal is what might best be termed the "political." The fundamental and astounding fact about this aspect of this ancient Cretan culture is that it endured, indeed flourished, for nearly one thousand years without any war. This phenomenon is frequently referred to as the "Pax Minoica," and it is so remarkable as to be nearly, quite literally, incredible. When one considers the fact that in all other civilizations, from other ancient peoples through the Middle Ages right down through modern Times, it would be difficult to find even a hundred year period of peace, this achievement of the Minoans stands out as perhaps the most significant in the history of humankind. The simple truth is that amongst all of the archaeological data pertaining to high Minoan culture so far excavated there is not any reference to battles, no representations of warriors of any sort, and not a single fortification. Moreover, when ever their contemporaries refer to the Minoans in their records there is never any mention of conflict.

Although a great many daggers, double axes, and pictures of sheilds have been found, the vast majority of these are clearly ceremonial in nature, while others appear to be most likely designed for hunting. Even domestically, there is no indication of internal conflict, even though there are at least a half dozen palaces and/or royal villas. Since none of these show any sign of a concern of defence, scholars have concluded that either there existed no civil conflict amongst the rulers or the different areas, or there was but one ruler who had several different palaces. In both cases, however, there is no gain-saying the fact that the Minoans enjoyed a prosperous and peaceful existence for close to one thousand years. As one comtemplates the natural beauty of Crete, together with the high level of aesthetic sensitivity and technological accomplishments of the Minoans, within the context of virtually perpetual peace, the combined result is perhaps truly beyond comprehension. If ever there was a utopian existence, this must have been it.

The natural question arising from a consideration of the fore going facts is" 'How did they do it?" Perhaps a brief reconsideration of some of the factors already discussed, will yield at least some clues as to the answer to this question. In the absence of any real written records from the thousand years between 2500 and 1500 B.C., we are left with but two possible sources as a basis for conjectures about the nature of political life in Minoan times. First, there are some written records in Linear B, along with the earliest European law-code at Gortys, inscribed around 450 B.C. but incorporating earlier material. From these documents, which Cretan life after the Mycenaean and Dorian invasions respectively, it is possible to gain some insight into what civil and social life in Crete was like after Minoan times. However, since the arrival of these warring peoples destroyed the very essence of the Minoan acheivement, these records are of no real help.

Secondly, Homer describes certain aspects of Cretan life at the time of the Trojan War, perhaps around 1250 B.C., but since he wrote at least several hundred years after this time, and since even this date is at least two hundred years after the demise of the Minoan culture, there is very little reason to think that Homer's descriptions are at all relevant to Minoan politics. The same must be said for the remarks of Herodotus and Aristotle, who wrote about Cretan politics in the fourth century B.C., several hundred years after Homer. Throughout all of these centuries the domestic politics of Crete were dominated by wars and threats of war, treties and some humanitarian laws, according to the familiar patterns of adversarial relations. This was a far cry from the "Pax Minoica" that characterized the culture of Crete between 2500 and 1500 B.C. In fact, most scholars agree with Aristotle's description of post-Minoan Crete as essentially similar to Sparta in political and military organization.

So, once again, we must return to the simple facts regarding the complete absence of any of the trappings of war throughout the years of high Minoan culture. There simply is no indication of any conflict or even preparation for possible conflict in all that has been uncovered in Minoan Crete or the surrounding islands from this time period. Surely part of the explanation stems from the fact that Crete was an island civilization, separated from the surrounding mainlands of Europe, Asia Minor, and North Africa by nearly two hundred miles in every direction. However, since the Minoans were extensive seafareres, this comparative isolation cannot be the sole cause of their tranquil existence. At least part of the answer to this puzzle would seem to lie in the joyous and optimistic Minoan spirit, which has been described by Professor Nikos Platon, in his book Crete, as one which took "delight in beauty, grace, and movement, in the enjoyment of life and closeness to nature" (pp 148 and 143).

Professor Platon goes on to indicate that there seems to have been an equitable sharing of wealth in the Minoan society, for even though there existed a ruling class which enjoyed palatial living, throughout Crete "The standard of living-even of peasants-seems to have been high...None of the homes found so far have suggested very poor living conditions" (p. 178). Another abvious but often overlooked factor operative within Minoan political life is the prominent role played by women. Everywhere in the murals and frescoes, even in the highly athletic and dangerous "bull-games," we see women as full participants in public life. Given the fact that a chief, if not the chief deity was the Earth or Mother Goddess, it is not at all far-fetched to suggest that women also played an equal role in Minoan government. As professor Platon puts it: "The whole of life was pervaded by an ardent faith in the goddess Nature, the source of all creation and harmony. This led to a love of peace, a horror of tyranny, and a respect for the law. Even among the ruling classes personal ambition seems to have been unknown; nowhere do we find the name of an author attached to a work of art nor a record of the deeds of a ruler" (p. 148).

Without wishing to support every aspect of her work, I tend to agree with Riane Eisler that there is a surprizing correlation between the decline of Minoan culture, including the demise of "Pax Minoica," and the rise of more militarily-minded, aggressive societies. More pointedly, since Minoan culture was characterized by the prominance of women in religion, politics, and art, while the more war-like peoples were dominated by male leaders, it surely seems to follow that the culturally rich and peaceful quality of Minoan culture was directly tied to the equal, if not superior, role played by women. Although nearly all male scholars in this field begin by acknowledging the centrality of women in Minoan art, religion, and politics, they invariably fail to see any connection between this and the unique quality of this ancient Cretan civilization. As Eisler says in her book, The Chalice and the Blade:

> They may note that, in sharp contrast to other ancient and contemporary civilizations, in Crete the "feminine" virtues of peaceableness and sensitivity to the needs of others were given social priority. And they may also note that in contrast to other societies, Cretan women had high social, economic, political, and religious positions. But they do so only in passing, with no emphasis, thus signaling to the reader receptive to their authority that this is an ancillary or peripheral matter (p. 39-40).

Thus, the most likely answer to our original question, "How did the Minoans acheive nearly a thousand year peace?" would seem to lie in the equality of the sexes in both religion and every aspect of public life, together with a sense of harmony with nature, a general sharing of wealth, and a deep appreciation of aesthetic activity. While one cannot help but be inspired by this concrete array of humanistic values in Minoan culture, it is difficult not to become depressed by the fact that nearly every aspect of modern Western culture is directly opposed to the realization of these humane qualities. In my own opinion, although our currenty society continues to pay lif-service to these aspirations, it systematically undermines them by its emphasis on individual gain and material success. These latter values can only engender exploitations, alienation, and narrow nationalism. It has become clear by this time of day that there exists a desparate need on planet earth for the qualities that enabled the Minoans to acheive a lasting peace.

Although Crete is not known for its role in the development of classical Greek culture, nor as the home of any of the important ruins thereof, my own encounter with it has taken place against the backdrop of the Greek heritage. Not only was I originally drawn to Crete in connection with my study of ancient Greek philosophy and civilizations, but over the years of teaching and bringing students to Greece and Crete, the two cultures have become connected in my experience. Moreover, there are many interesting comparisons and contrasts that can be drawn between the two ancient societies, especially in the fields of art, politics, and religion. In this chapter I shall briefly review some of the salient features of the classical Greek heritage, focusing specifically on its contributions to our Western understanding of the relationship between body and mind. Along the way I shall offer some of my own reflections on this heritage as it relates to that of the Minoans and to contemporary Crete.

As the Minoans seem to have sprung up on Crete without any antecedents, so the classical Greek culture seems to have arrived on the scene pretty much out of nowhere. There was a kind of "dark ages" between the fall of Minoan culture and the rise of classical Greece, dominated by Mycenaeans, Dorians, and the other northern marauders. Homer's Iliad and Hesiod's Theogeny are generally dated around 1800 and 1000 B.C. respectively. It is from these two books, along with Homer's Odyssey, a collection of "Homeric Hymns," and the poems of Pindar, that the Greek mythological heritage derives. By the time of the great Greek playwrights, historians, and philosophers, namely between 500 and 350 B.C., the main foundations of Greek culture had been laid. The pantheon, from Zeus on down, was in place and the Trojan War, with all its subplots, had become common folklore.

It is possible to understand the rise of classical culture as the effort of ancient Greek people to find or construct an ordered pattern, or rationale, within the chaos of both physical and human existence. Their key move in this effort was to place humankind at the center of the universe, as the most important element in it. Unlike the Minoans, who saw themselves as part and parcel of the broader natural world, the Greeks came to see themselves as unique in the world, as capable of shaping their own lives and their own destiny. To be sure, this shaping was understood as limited by the parameters of time, fate, and death, but within these limits there was ample room to order one's life and world in such a way as to ensure a full and meaningful existence.

Even the gods of the ancient Greeks were conceived in the image of humans, rather than the other way around. Not only did they bear no likeness whatsoever to various animals or birds, as did the gods of all other ancient peoples, but the Greek gods gradually came to take on the ideal characteristics to which the Greeks themselves aspired, namely rationality, beauty, and justice. For the Greeks, life and the world could be understood and ordered so as to enhance their positive aspects and minimize terror and chaos. Thus it was that Greek religion had no official priesthood or Orthodox dogma through which to dictate and limit the beliefs and practices of the people. Even the gods sometimes failed to achieve the ultimate Greek goal of "excellence," and were judged or laughed at accordingly. Moreover, astronomers, philosophers, and artists alike were free to explore and speculate in whatever way they wished, as long as they strove for rationality and justice. Edith Hamilton summarizes this revolutionary beginning of classical culture in the following words:

> *People often speak of the Greek miracle. What the phrase tries to express is the new birth of the world with the awakening of Greece. Old things are passed away; behold, all things are become new. Something like that happened in Greece. Why it happened, or when, we have no idea at all. We know only that in the earliest Greek poets a new point of view dawned, never dreamed in the world before them, but never to leave the world after them. With the coming forward of Greece, mankind became the center of the universe, the most important thing in it. This was a revolution in thought. Human beings had counted for little heretofore. In Greece man first realized what mankind was"* (p. 7-8).

The high period of classical Greek culture, what is often termed the "Golden Age," was formed in the crucible of war, between the battles with the Persians in 480 B.C. and the Peloponnesian wars

Epidaurus Theater

ending in 412-404 B.C. Prior to the invasion of the Persians, the main city-states of Greece had arisen and continued as essentially independent political entities. The major cities, Athens, Corinth, and Sparta were drawn together into a loose federation in order to repulse the Persians, only to see this unity collapse in the civil wars amongst themselves, which Sparta won in 404 B.C. Although the Greek

Dionysian Theater Athens

way of life was perpetuated and perpetrated on others by the expansion of Alexander The Great's empire, the "glory that was Greece" had been dissipated well before the time of his death in 323 B.C. In the meantime, however, the citizens of Athens, who had played the most strategic role in the victory over the Persians, found themselves swept forward by a fresh confidence which transformed the groping humanism of the late archaic period into what we know as classical Greek culture.

Pericles was, of course, both the embodiment of and the catalyst for the spirit of Greek's "Golden Age." Between 460 and his death in 429 B.C., Pericles led Athens to its zenith as a political power and cultural ideal. In 448 he finalized a peace treaty with Persia and took control of the Delian League which was originally formed among the Aegean islands as a defense against the Persians. Also, by means of speeches and gigantic public building projects, culminating in the Acropolis, Pericles built Greek pride and confidence in its own worth and destiny. He also initiated the world's first democratic government. This brief burst of cultural prosperity and domestic tranquility soon gave way to the deteriorations of the thirty year war with Sparta, culminating in the defeat of Athens in 404 and the trial and death of Socrates in 399 B.C. The ideals of this Periclean Golden Age are well focused in Professor Pollitt's summary, in his book <u>Art and Experience in Classical Greece</u>, of Pericles' most famous speech: "Athens is depicted as the one society where justice applies equally to all and where social restrictions do not prevent a man from becoming as great in public life as his natural capacity permits; submission to law and authority and acceptance of the dangers of war are maintained voluntarily, without force and without complaint; power and discipline are balanced by a free intellectual life and a buoyant spirit; the functioning of the society is open for all to see; neither all societies, the 'school of Hellas'" (P. 68).

Professor Pollitt goes on to develop a most interesting theory concerning the causal relation between this new Greek Spirit and the art of the classical period. He suggests that the confidence arising from the victory over the Persians was offset by a fresh

Parthenon

sense of the requirements of justice, and that the juxtaposition of these two qualities produced the dynamic sense of balance and proportion that characterized the "classical movement." This mixture of grandeur and movement, of order and action, is very clearly embodied in the Parthenon and the wonderful statue of Poseidon, for example. Pollitt argues that witnessing the Persians being punished for their imperialistic arrogance flavored the newly discovered Greek confidence sufficiently, if only momentarily, to keep them from becoming over-confident. He thinks the Oresteia trilogy by Aeschylus, in which Orestes is acquitted by Athena in order to put an end to the cycle of vengeance as a means of "justice," served to formalize this new vision of rational, impartial justice.

It is both interesting and instructive to compare and contrast classical Greek and Minoan cultures at this juncture. Although both seem to have achieved a high sense of self-confidence and prosperity, the Minoan achievement lasted far longer and was not born of war. Furthermore, although the Minoans were ruled by a royal class of some type, their political system seems to have been a stable and equitable one, lasting as it did for many hundreds of years without any indication of inner military conflict. They, too, would appear to have effected a dynamic balance between confidence and responsibility, one which is also reflected in their art and religion. A remarkable difference, and quite a puzzling one, between the two cultures is that the Minoans were able to accomplish this without a written language, while for the Greeks, their literary and philosophical tradition was one of the primary vehicles of their cultural achievement. Art was, of course, crucial to the rise and richness of the Minoans and Greeks alike, as were athletic contests.

While Minoan art was focused in painting, pottery, jewelry, and architecture, classical Greek art has come down to us primarily in the form of pottery, sculpture, and architecture. Although the Greeks did in fact paint, even painting their marble statues and buildings, almost none of these have survived the centuries. The Greeks, too, were almost exclusively representational, focusing however primarily on the human form and only secondarily on animal life. They also employed a good deal of formal geometric design, especially on their vases, reinforced by various patterns of red and black. In addition to being nearly exclusively narrational in form, in some way depicting a scene or pose from a well-known myth or historic event, Greek representational art was generally quite idealized and stylized. Thus the subjects appear as far more physically stiff and formal in posture than those we see in Minoans paintings and statuettes.

Professor Pollitt's theory is that during the "classical moment" of the Golden Age of Pericles (450-430 B.C.) one can see a shift to a more human, more realistic portrayal of human beings, heros and gods. He traces this refined humanism to the new found confidence tempered with justice mentioned previously. Furthermore, Pollitt contends that this fresh realism gave way to a kind of baroque "mannerism" as the classical culture began to deteriorate after Pericles' death. There are those who suggest that this pattern often arises when people are seeking to stabilize themselves by reaffirming a tradition to the point of saturation in a time of political breakup. Finally, Pollitt says the last phase of

classical Greek culture is represented by the individualism and eclecticism of the time of the great philosophers and the final burst of imperial glory embodied in the reign of Alexander the Great (400-322 B.C.).

This same general development from archaic times to the Golden Age can be traced in the patterns of Greek temple architecture. The temple of Zeus at Olympia,

Athena Tholos Delphi

Temple of Apollo Delphi

completed around 460 B.C., expresses the newly found confidence of the Early classical period in its colossal severity and control, even as does the famous charioteer at Delphi. The Parthenon, on the other hand, stands as the paradigmatic expression of the classic Greek glorification of self-confidence, as a tour-de-force of the human creation of beauty through the control of line, shape, and proportion. It was constructed between 447 and 432 B.C., at the height of Pericles' Golden Age. In the decades after the "classical moment" temple architecture took on a far more eclectic and awkward character, as can be seen in the temple of Apollo of Bassae and in the Erechtheion on the Athenian Acropolis. The latter was completed in 406 B.C., just prior to Athens defeat by Sparta. Down through this fourth century B.C. the majority of public monuments honored great, historical leaders rather than gods and legendary heroes.

Additional and insightful light is shed on Greek architecture by Professor Rhys Carpenter in his book The Aesthetic Basis of Greek Art. He begins with the observation that architecture actually represents a fourth dimension in space, since it encloses an area rather than simply being in one, as is the case with sculpture. Carpenter continues by suggesting that the Greek temples really deal with the organization of rectangular planes in space rather than with solid figures as one might suppose. The combination of thin atmosphere and bright light in Greece, on the one hand, and the soft, light surfaces of marble, on the other, tends to make the temples appear flat and ethereal. He surmises that it was this set of circumstances that initiated the use of fluted columns in the temples, to provide shadows and a sense of solidarity.

Carpenter also thinks that throughout the entire Greek period there was a surprising lack of creativity in design shown by the archite-cts. He attributes this "monotony" to the fact that while representational artists found their models in great variety all around them, the first architects had to create their non-representational

Korinthian Columns Korinthos

models from ide as alone. Thus the three famous "orders" of Greek architecture, the Doric, the Ionian, and the Corinthian, were rather slavishly copied after they had been established, just as animals and humans were repeatedly copied by representational artists.

Professor Carpenter summarizes what he takes to be the unique character of architecture in relation to human experience in the following remarks:

We are always external to sculpture, but the works of architecture enclose us spatially, hem us in and ring us round with vast masses of stone many times our height and weight. Not only de we crane our heads, focus our eyes for distance, perform actual physical exertion in moving from point to point; but we are at the mercy of suggestions of confinement, freedom of movement, oppression, physical danger. Our eyes travel up with us easily to vast heights, or struggle hopelessly over the horizontal barriers which keep us down. We have vast cisterns of air to breathe, or our lungs gasp under the illusion that we are closely shut in. There is, indeed, an entire range of bodily experiences, for the most part not very prominent in our consciousness, to which the formal suggestions of architecture may appeal. Such are our sense of pose and bodily balance, of muscular self-control, accuracy of movement, lightness and agility, feelings of strength and self-assurance, freedom of breath, even such vague bodily states as accompany security of footing, indifference to external forces, determination and endurance, boldness and fatigue (p. 147-148).

In reflecting on Carpenter's analysis of Greek architecture, as well as his interesting account of Greek sculpture, there is one point of convergence with many of the points made by Professor Pollitt which I find especially fascinating. Moreover, this point of convergence in the works of these two scholars intersects quite forcefully with a particular aspect of my own experience and thought. What I have in mind here is the specific way in which the classical Greeks integrated the physical and mental dimensions of human experience. Throughout all my travels in and study of Greece I have been most consistently impressed with the unique synthesis of body and mind that we find expressed in the art of the classical age. In terms that resonate with his kinesthetic analysis of architecture quoted above, Carpenter speaks of this synthesis in terms of the geometric formula which enabled the best of the Greek sculptors to control the poses of their statues so as to provide "the extraordinary completeness of each aspect under which the statue can be viewed...and the remarkably harmonious manner in which each aspect arises out of the preceding and melts into the succeeding one, as we move around the statue" (p. 62-63).

Pollitt speaks in a similar manner of how the great sculptures of the classical moment exhibit "a visible harmony of counterbalancing forces achieved by arranging the parts of the body in a chiastic scheme" (p. 108) in which the continuous spiral of the posture reflects a perfect balance of motion and stability. What is striking here is the combination of intellectual and somatic understanding of human embodied experience. Moreover, our own appreciation or apprehension of the statue is also both mental and physical, though directly, not as a matter of inference from the latter by means of and to the former. Here is how Professor Carpenter puts it:

Still, there is some very clear connection between our apprehension of the solid as solid in the case of a human statue and the fact that the only other method of direct apprehension of spatial solidity is our awareness of it for our own body. It may not be strictly our own strength or power of movement or agility or gravitational equilibrium which we feel to be heightened while we contemplate the sculptural indication of these qualities; but our power of spatially apprehending the statue as we spatially apprehend our own bodily selves makes us immensely susceptible and sympathetic to an emotional and almost muscular-physical understanding of such qualities when they are sculpturally presented. We know them, not from the outside (as we comprehend strength when we see a strong man pull or push or lift, as we comprehend speed when we watch runners, or agility as when we see a mountain-goat but from the inside, in terms of what they are for their possessor (pp. 69-70).

This fascination with the integration of mind and body is not only characteristic of the art of the Classical Greeks, but is exhibited as well in their love of athletics. Although the Greeks can be compared to the Minoans in their love of games and the depiction thereof,

Delphi Stadium

there is no comparison in their respective treatment of human bodily activity. Minoan figures are indeed graceful in their simplicity, but Greek sculptures combine such grace with a powerful realism and a deep intellectual understanding of the geometric principles involved in both human embodiment and its artistic portrayal. It is perhaps the hallmark of classical Greek culture that it sought, and to a grand degree achieved, a dynamic balance between body and mind. This achievement was lived and honored within the ceremonial patterns of their games and festivals, as well as within their art and their politics. Ever since childhood, when I did my first report of the Olympic Games, right up to my present study of Greek art and philosophy, this particular integration of the mind and body has remained a source of deep fascination for me.

What is peculiar about this Classical Greek integration of the mental and the physical in art is that it did not continue on into the thought of those Greek philosophers often classified as the greatest of all, namely, Socrates, Plato, and Aristotle. Although there were philosophers active during the entire classical period, the real beginning point for philosophy must be centered in the trial and death of Socrates in 399 B.C. Socrates himself never wrote any of his ideas down, preferring to philosophize daily in the marketplace among his fellow citizens. It was left to Plato, his most brilliant student, to provide posterity with an account of Scorates' philosophical concerns and methods in his early dialogues, such as <u>Apology</u>, <u>Crito</u>, <u>Phaedo</u>, and <u>Euthyphro</u>. In his more mature work, such as the <u>Republic</u>, Plato developed his own philosophical posture and doctrines which were in many ways quite different from those of Socrates.

Socrates had lived through the entire classical period and had participated fully in the fruits of Pericles' Golden Age, especially in the political democracy it provided. However, after Athens was finally defeated in its thirty year war with Sparta in 404 B.C., the newly established puppet-government found it convenient to find scapegoats by means of which to explain the recent collapse of the classical age and sought to purge Athens of those who would hinder their work of maintaining the status quo. Unfortunately, because of his commitment to discovering the

Traditional site of Socrates Imprisonment

truth through a process of relentless question-asking, Socrates was perceived by certain people to be a subversive element in the Athenian community. His trial appears to have been an attempt to shut him up, but when Socrates refused to cease his search for truth, or to apologize for having motivated others to seek the truth, the trial culmuminated in Socrates being sentenced to death. Refusing the opportunity to escape from prison, he died with dignity and without regrets, thereby insuring his place in history as a martyr in the continual struggle for freedom and justice.

Plato went on to develop his own philosophy against the backdrop of Socrates personal inspiration and political "failure." He believed that the dialogical method which Socrates employed was, indeed, the only way to reach the truth, but he concluded that this method can only be successful when used by gifted thinkers who have undergone rigorous mathematical and philosophical training. Once such "philosopher kings" were in a position of leadership, they could, according to Plato's dream, construct a harmonious society based on truth and justice, a true "Republic." Socrates mistake, then, was in trying to practice the search for truth among a people who had no appreciation for what this search involved. Thus it was that Plato had little patience for the Perclean ideal of democracy, for a true understanding of justice will come only to those who are intelligent and trained enough to grasp it. Uneducated commoners are not in a position to do justice, simply because they cannot know justice.

In the Republic, Plato likened the philosopher's search to the journey of a person from the bottom of a deep shadowy cave up and out into the light of reality. By asking questions which push beyond appearances, the searcher first learns to distinguish the laws governing contingent physical and social reality from mere hear-say and prejudice. Then, by means of the study of the eternal laws of mathematics, especially geometry, one acquires the skills necessary to the comprehension of the higher conceptual ideals, or "Forms" as Plato called them, from which everything in the natural world derives its existence. It is, of course, the sun that both gives life to these paradigms of reality and renders them "visible" to the understanding. In Plato's allegory of The Cave, the sun stands for the "Form of the Good," the conceptual reality at the apex of the entire pyramid of all that is. Once a searcher has reached the realm of the Forms, and comprehended the Form of Justice, he or she is in a position to return to the everyday world and rule. Once established as rulers, independent thought and public opinion would not be tolerated, since the truth would now be known.

Like Socrates, Plato lived in very unstable times politically speaking, and he made several unsuccessful efforts to persuade Dion, the ruler of Syracuse, to implement his utopian ideals. Finally, he resigned himself to propagating his doctrines through his writings and the school he established in Athens, the "Academy." The most outstanding student in this school was Aristotle, who studied with Plato for twenty years. Having grown up in the home of a doctor, Aristotle was far more empirically minded than Plato, preferring the inductive accumulation of information to the deductive demonstration of geometry. Being from the northern province of Macedonia, he served for several years as the tutor of young Alexander the Great. Later in life Aristotle founded a school of his own in Athens, called the "Lyceum." When Alexander's father, King Philip became a threat to Athens and its surrounding city-states, Aristotle came under increasing suspicion as a potential collaborator. He finally went into self-imposed exile, "lest Athens sin against philosophy a second time."

Although his philosophy was similar to Plato's in many respects, Aristotle differed in his understanding of the relationship between formal reality and the natural world. Unlike Plato, he thought that the Forms or ideal concepts do not exist independently of their concrete, individual instances. While "Redness" or "Treeness," for instance, can be distinguished from specific instances of red and particular trees in abstract analysis, they can not, according to Aristotle, either subsist or be known independently of them. This means that even the Form of Justice can only be known by means of a thorough examination of the various concrete cases wherein it is more or less embodied. Thus, rather than construct an ideal society on the basis of abstract reasoning, as did his mentor, Aristotle preferred to move toward a deeper understanding of Justice through an empirical and inductive analysis of the constitutions of the various states of his day.

With respect to politics in particular, Aristotle was every bit as aristocratic as Plato, believing that only certain people have what it takes to rule and that slaves are absolutely necessary to the smooth running of any prosperous state. He, too, shunned democracy as a poor substitute for real political leadership. It must be remembered, however, that theirs was an aristocracy of intelligence and wisdom, not blood, tradition, or money. Their elitism was essentially an elitism of knowledge, not class, power, or race. Although this political posture has its obvious drawbacks, it somehow seems less wrong-headed when viewed against the backdrop of contemporary America, in which the Jeffersonian ideal of the democratic rule of an educated populous has been eroded by materialism and the mass media into a demogogory of popularity.

Perhaps the strongest criticism that can be leveled against the sort of intellectual elitism advocated by these thinkers and especially by Plato, is that in their ideal society there would be no room for the likes of Socrates, the "gad fly" whose role was to keep rulers on their toes. As Winston Churchill said, "Democracy is absolutely the worst form of government, except for all the rest."

When we think of the great classical age of ancient Greece, we generally conflate the achievement of Pericles and the many great artists and writers of the period between 480 and 404 B.C. with the great philosophers of the following century. It is extremely significant, however, that not only did Socrates, Plato, and Aristotle live for the most part after the "Golden Age" of Greece, but for the most part they stood against the ideals of this period, as well. We have already seen how this was so with respect to the political ideas of democracy and independent thought. In addition, however, to a large degree, they also moved away from the classical ideal of the integration of the mental and physical dimensions of human experience. A brief examination of how this is so will lead us directly to the very heart of the philosophies of these thinkers.

As a participant in the Periclean Golden Age, Socrates was naturally enculturated to believe and live the classical ideal of body and mind as two sides of the same coin. Not only had he taken part in various and vigorous military expeditions as a younger man, but in the Symposium Plato portrays him as capable of drinking his comrades under the table during an all night philosophical discussion and walking away in the morning. In addition, it is known that he had recently fathered a child at the time of his death, at the age of 70. More importantly, Socrates' philosophy itself inherently involved an active integration of body and mind, since the primary thrust of his questioning process was aimed at achieving <u>knowledge</u> of how to <u>live</u> better. His most famous saying is: "The unexamined life is not worth living." Socrates sought knowledge, not as an end in itself, but as a means to becoming a better person.

Nevertheless, to the extent that Socrates believed that "knowledge is virtue," that it is essentially impossible for a person knowingly to do what is counter productive to their own good, to this extent he suggested that a knowledge of what is right is sufficient. This idea may have served as the seed for Plato's tendency to equate cognition with he intellectual process of philosophical dialogue. At any rate, it becomes perfectly clear that as he developed his overall philosophy, Plato paid little attention to the role of human embodiment in the search for truth and the good life. Although in the <u>Republic</u> he begins his account of an ideal education by devoting several years to both gymnastics and music accompanied by movement, he soon has the student move on to more intellectual enterprises. In so doing, Plato implies that at the most the role of the body is preliminary to that of the mind, while at the least it is secondary to it.

At the heart of Plato's philosophy there is a fundamental dichotomy between mind and body. He often speaks of the body as "the prison of the soul" and of the mind as "the eye of the soul." Most likely this negative posture toward embodiment drives from the correlation of his distrust of sense perception and his enamorment of geometry. Because claims to knowledge of sensation often turn out to be mistaken, and because mathematical precision can guarantee certainty, Plato denigrated the one and committed himself to the other. Even in dreams and hallucinations, two plus two equals four. Likewise, since sense perception is based in the body and mathematical processes are essentially conceptual, it follows that the former can only hinder the latter and most therefore be avoided. Thus a strong wedge was driven between the body and the mind in Plato's philosophy.

There is, perhaps, no more vivid image of this dichotomy between body and mind in Plato's writings than that of the chariot drawn by two horses and driven by a charioteer. In Plato's description, the two horses represent the aspects of human embodiment, the appetites and the emotions, while the charioteer represents the rationally mind. Although the horses are acknowledged as necessary for pulling the chariot, they must be controlled and guided by reason if the chariot is to function smoothly and effectively. Clearly, for Plato, the mind is what gives human beings their distinctive character as "rational animals" and renders cognition possible. He even has Socrates insist, just prior to drinking the fatal cup of hemlock at his execution, that true lovers of wisdom welcome death as an escape from the body into the realm of truth, beauty, and, goodness, a kind of "conceptual heaven."

It is possible to make a case for the conclusion that the key to Plato's approach to the disrelation between body and mind is his choice of visual experience as the paradigm of knowledge. In spite of the obvious irony involved in such a choice, given his negative attitude toward sense perception as a source of knowledge, Plato's crucial allegory of the cave depends upon it. Indeed, throughout his writings, Plato continually employs the image of true cognition as a kind of unhindered vision of Formal reality. In the bottom of the cave, which represents the confinement of bodily existence and sensory perception, the would-be knower is the victim of imagination and guess-work. By following the light of reason, however, the potential knower first advances to the general intellectual principles of science, then to the eternal conceptual truths of mathematics, and finally to the ideals of Formal reality. Here is how Plato himself summarizes his central image:

> The realm of the visible should be compared to the prison dwelling, and the fire inside it to the power of the sun. If you interpret the upward journey and the contemplation of things above as the upward journey of the soul to the intelligible realm, you will grasp what I surmise since you were keen to hear it. Whether it is true or not only the god knows, but this is how I see it, namely that in the intelligible world the Form of the Good is the last to be seen, and with difficulty; when seen it must be reckoned to be for all the cause of all that is right and beautiful, to have produced in the visible world both light and the fount of light, while in the intelligible world it is itself that which produces and controls truth and intelligence, and he who

is to act intelligently in public or in private must see it.
(p.170).

The chief difficulty with this understanding of knowledge would seem to be that it <u>begins</u> by separating the knower from what is to be known. Once this separation is established it becomes virtually impossible to overcome it, for it is always possible to ask whether one actually has achieved a completely accurate view or understanding of the reality in question. Although Plato believed that a completely accurate knowledge was attainable through abstract reasoning, the entire history of Western philosophy, right up to the present, can be understood as a debate over whether and how such knowledge is possible. Many philosophers have argued that although it is possible to gain certainty through rational abstraction, the price one pays such knowledge is that it is of necessity empty of factual content. These thinkers contend that all such knowledge, like that of mathematics, is based on stipulative definitions and deductive reasoning, and as such only yields conclusions which have been built in at the outset.

Perhaps an example is called for here. If we say "all bachelors are happy," the truth of this statement depends on obtaining factual data about the emotional state of bachelors. At best such date can establish the truth of the statement to a high degree of probability, since it only takes one happy bachelor to make it false. On the other hand, if we say "all bachelors are unmarried males," the truth of this statement is not dependent on data about bachelors, but on the definitions of the terms involved. Thus the statement is necessarily true, but it is empty of any information about the world, since it is true even if at the moment there are no bachelors. Therefore, even though factual knowledge is only highly probable at best, the price for obtaining certainty is factual emptiness.

More centrally related to our original concern here, however, is the inadvisability of setting up or following a philosophy that requires a separation of the two distinctive dimensions of human existence, body and mind. Although it is admittedly extremely difficult to comprehend the inner workings of the intricate relationship between these two equally important aspects of our experience, any theory which seeks to separate them flies in the face of perhaps the most fundamental fact of all of life. The simple truth is that however it is to be understood, the reciprocal interaction and interdependency between thought and action stands as the very axis of both human behavior and consciousness. Our actions are informed by our minds and our thoughts are rooted in our bodies, even as speech both expresses and creates thought. The relationship between body and mind is fundamentally one of symbiosis, not separation.

Another concrete example or two may prove helpful here. Although nearly everyone can either move or not move the little finger on their left hand, no one can explain the mental difference between moving and not moving the finger. Or, to put it the other way around, we can of course, say that certain brain cells initiate an electrical impulse through a chain of synapses, and so on. However, there simply is no way to speak about how the <u>thought</u>, of moving one's little finger gets transposed into <u>physical</u> brain cells. Yet we engage in such reciprocal interplay literally millions of times every day. In the same way, our recognition of a familiar face in a huge crowd of people, or the strains of a long-forgotten song, to say nothing of our grasp of our own natural language, is anchored in but not strictly limited to the somatic judgments made by our senses. We <u>know</u> a great many things, such as where our own center of gravity is, which we are unable to articulate conceptually.

In addition to being wrong-headed as a theory of cognition, Plato's mind-body dualism gives rise to an unhealthy view of human values and relationships. For, not only is bodily health and activity vital to human happiness and productivity, but there is strong contemporary indication that rational activity is far more anchored in and mediated by our embodiment than was formerly imagined. It should be sufficient merely to mention psycho-somatic medicine and the "imaging" technique in sport psychology. Likewise, when the symbiotic interaction between mind and body is denied or ignored, all sorts of debilitating social tendencies are set in motion. Indeed, many of the cultural schizophrenia of modern times, such as that reflected in our inability to develop a healthy attitude toward sexuality, may well be traceable to our society's long tradition of separating the physical from the mental.

It is because of the foregoing difficulties that I find it more helpful to turn to the philosophy of Plato's greatest student, Aristotle, when reflecting on the relation between mind and body. While Aristotle for the most part agreed with Plato that intellectual activity is the distinctive characteristic and highest achievement of human life, we have already seen that he differed from him with respect to the inter-relatedness of Formal reality and material existence. Moreover, Aristotle maintained that our conceptual knowledge arises out of our perceptual knowledge by virtue of the capacity to grasp the similarities and differences amongst the individual physical entities which we encounter. By encountering a number of instances of blue, for example, a child comes to <u>recognize</u> the idea of blueness. Thus for Aristotle, although simple perceptual exposure is insufficient to yield knowledge, it is absolutely necessary in order to activate rational thought. This necessity, however, is not merely one of providing data from which to infer more general concepts, but is rather one of mediating conceptual understanding in the same way as a catalyst brings about a chemical alteration. In both cases that which mediates is actually incorporated into the resultant reality. Here is how Aristotle summarizes it:

> *We conclude that these states of knowledge are neither innate in a determinate form, nor developed from other higher states of knowledge, but from sense-perception. It is like a rout in battle stopped by first one man making a stand and then another, until the original formation has been restored. The soul is so constituted as to be capable of this process.*

When we turn to Aristotle's approach to morality we can see his effort to integrate mind and body even more clearly. He begins by insisting that virtue is not an abstract quality which attaches first to persons and then causally to their behavior. Rather, Aristotle claims, virtue is a matter of character and disposition embodied in a person's mode of life, in their choices and habits. This character and these habits are acquired through a kind of "moral apprenticeship" in which one becomes a virtuous person by <u>doing</u> virtuous deeds. The possibility of such acquisition by apprenticeship is, of course, dependent on being encompassed by persons who both model virtuous behavior and instruct concerning it. What for Plato was the result of intellectual understanding of the concept of virtue or justice, became for Aristotle the product of practice and skill, involving the mind and body working together. Aristotle explains it thusly:

> Again, of all the things that come to us by nature we first acquire the potentiality and later exhibit the activity (this is plain in the case of the senses' for it was not by often seeing or often hearing that we got these senses, but on the contrary we
> had them before we used them, and did not come to have them by using them); but the virtues we get by first exercising them, as also happens in the case of the arts as well. For the things we have to learn before we can do them, we learn by doing them, e.g., men become builders by building and lyre players by playing the lyre; so too we become just by doing just acts, temperate by doing temperate acts, brave by doing brave acts.

More specifically, Aristotle analyzed moral virtue as the healthy balance between extreme forms of behavior. Courage, for instance, he defined as the balance or mid-point between cowardice and foolhardiness, while temperance is the balance between self-indulgence and asceticism, and so forth. This dynamic balance Aristotle termed the "Golden Mean" because he saw it as the key to the development of moral character. By following the virtuous example of others, and by striving to strike the proper balance between extremes with respect to each choice and each quality of character, a person develops moral skill and becomes virtuous. The "Golden Mean" is not, for Aristotle, an abstract concept statically applied to every situation and/or moral agent. It is, rather, a flexible balance, relative to the concrete situation. Aristotle says: "Virtue, then, is a state of character concerned with choice, lying in a mean, i.e., the mean relative to us, this being determined by a rational principle, and by that principle by which the man of practical wisdom would determine it" (p. 190).

Here, then, we see that for Aristotle virtue is an integration of rational judgment and bodily activity. This contrasts directly with Plato's notion of virtue as a result of conceptual knowledge, as well as with the traditional Western religious view that virtue is a matter of obeying specific commandments. This definition of virtue as a function of character also conflicts with the contemporary idea that virtue is either outmoded altogether, or that it equates with whatever "feels right." Contrary to what one might initially think, this way of understanding morality is far more demanding, as well as rewarding, than any of these other approaches. The patience, judgment, and skill involved in this holistic posture take both time, and effort, and they provide no easy solutions either. They do, however, ensure that a person's morality is responsible.

Aristotle's way of approaching these issues, both moral excellence in general and the relationship between body and mind in particular, seems much more akin to that of the Golden Age of Perielean Athens than does the approach developed by Plato. It is this integration of mental and physical activity, especially as encountered in the classical aesthetic, that has and continues to draw me to the achievement of Classical Greece. More over, from the vantage point provided by Crete, in both its Minoan and contemporary aspects, this classical heritage harmonizes extremely well with the social and personal contours of my own experience in and of Greece. In addition to having a deep appreciation for both the Minoan and Hellenic perspectives on human embodiment, as seen in their art and their love of athletics, I have always sought to interact with the physical dimensions of Greece as much as with its cultural heritage. Let me explain.

Since my own life has to a large degree been shaped by athletic activity and geographic travel, it has been quite natural and appropriate to continue in these modes whenever visiting Greece. Not only have I travelled by bus and car throughout the countryside of both mainland Greece and a number of islands, but I have been able to do a great deal of hiking and climbing in the mountains and along the beaches as well. In addition, traveling by boat back and forth across the Mediterranean, as well as frequently swimming it, has brought me closer to the Greek and Minoan experience as sea-faring peoples. Finally, in recent years I have been able to extend my own embodied encounter with Crete through sculpting its various stones and participating in countless informal basketball games. All such activity, especially when blended with a good deal of reading, writing, and teaching on Greek themes has served well to get me deeper into Greece and Greece deeper into me.

Many years after the demise of classical Greece, at the high point of the Roman Empire, Christianity became the "officially" religion of the West, with Constantinople as its capital. This shift marked a fundamental pivot point in the history of Greece as well as the rest of Europe. During the first few centuries of Christdome, all of the countries and cultures of the West, including what we know today as Russia, were reshaped to fit into the religious categories introduced through the Apostle Pauls' interpretation of the life and teachings of Jesus, a Hebrew. In addition, nearly the whole known world was reshaped to fit into political categories borrowed from the Roman Empire. Down through these first several centuries, a good deal of tension developed between those who continued to think of Rome as the center of the Christian "Empire" and those who had adopted Constantinople as the center. One important reason for this growing rift was that those in the West used Latin as their official language, while those in the East used Greek.

Finally, around 1,000 A.D., the two factions split into two essentially distinct entities, the Roman Catholic church and the Eastern Orthodox church. The Greek and the Russian cultures, along with the Balkan culture, continued to develop a version of the Christian faith which became quite different from both the Catholic church and its Protestant off-spring. In Greece this faith runs very deep and effects nearly everything. Thus it is that one cannot come to an understanding of traditional Greek culture without acquiring a basic acquaintance with its incorporation of Christianity. Although space will not permit anything close to a detailed account of the beliefs and practices of the Orthodox Church, a brief outline of these will prove helpful. While such themes and concerns are not specifically a part of the "Classical Heritage," they do form an essential dimension of what constitutes traditional Greek culture today. More pointedly, they relate directly to the question of the relationship between the physical and mental, or spiritual, dimensions of human experience.

During the first few centuries of Christendom, Augustine was the dominant theological figure. His particular blend of biblical teachings and Platonic doctrines formed the intellectual foundation for all theological thought until around 1200 A.D., well after the split between the East and the West. Augustine took the position that while faith and reason are both important, one must "first believe in order to understand." This somewhat "mystical" posture became and has been remained the backbone of the Orthodox faith down through the centuries. The Western Roman Catholic church, on the other hand, eventually chose the more rationalistic theological posture developed by Thomas Aquinas, which was in turn based on Aristotle's philosophy. Thus the emphasis in Orthodoxy has been and is on living one's life within the patterns and traditions of the church, which were revealed by God and propagated by the Church Fathers, rather than on thinking too much about the fine points of theological doctrine.

The two major issues, in addition to the natural cultural and linguistic differences involved, over which the Eastern and Western churches split may seem a bit trivial to modern day people. The first concerned the authority of the Pope and the second pertained to the triune nature of God. The Orthodox church does not accept the idea that Christendom should have one absolute leader; it prefers a sort of federation of the bishops of the various regions, or "Patriarchates," amongst which the position of leadership rotates. With respect to the doctrine of the Trinity, Roman Catholics taught that the Holy Spirit proceeds from Christ the Son, who in turn proceeds from the Father, while the Orthodox held that both the Holy Spirit and the Son proceed directly and equally from the Father. Over the centuries the Orthodox church has striven to keep itself pure of outside influences, and even though its churches in northern Europe and America have made a number of concessions to a more "modern" life style, the church as a whole has maintained an aloof attitude toward inter-church discussions and ecumenical mergers.

The basic doctrinal beliefs of the Orthodox Church are essentially the same as those of other major Christian denominations. The worship is extremely liturgical in that a great number of religious icons and rituals dominate the services. The all-male priesthood can and usually does marry, but only unmarried priests can become bishops. The large number of celebrations which constitute the church year and the necessary performance of specific sacraments govern the lives of the people to an astonishing degree, although this is less the case with the younger generations. In general the Orthodox church is a bit more lenient toward such issues as divorce, remarriage, and abortion than its Catholic counterpart, but it remains far more strict than mainline Protestant churches. I have, indeed, visited one Orthodox monastery near London which accepts both men and women, but which, nonetheless, requires the dissolution of their previous marriages.

An excellent book for further study is Timothy Ware's The Orthodox Church. Here is how he characterizes the church in which he has chosen to serve:

> *Orthodoxy claims to be universal - not exotic and oriental, but simple Christianity. Because of human failings and the accidents of history, the Orthodox Church has been largely restricted in the past to certain geographical areas. Yet to the Orthodox themselves their Church is something more than a group of local bodies. The word 'Orthodoxy' has the double meaning of 'right belief' and 'right glory' (or right worship'). The Orthodox, therefore, make what may seem at first a surprising claim: they regard their Church as the Church which guards and teaches the true belief about God and which glorifies Him with right worship, that is, **as nothing less than the Church on earth** (p. 16).*

In general posture there is something more "earthy" about the Orthodox faith than the more intellectual Roman Catholic church. Indeed, it was the strong emphasis on the enfleshment of Christ in Jesus of Nazareth that formed the basis for their prolific use of icons, statues, and frescoes. Since God saw fit to be embodied in material flesh, for all to see and touch, it seemed only appropriate for the church to do the same with visual and tactile representations. On the other hand, however, the mystical tendencies within Orthodox theological tradition militate as much against the importance of embodiment as they do against an emphasis on the life of the mind. This is especially true with respect to the traditional monastic movement, where the notion of withdrawal from "the world" and from "femaleness" is stressed very strongly. Also, in the worship service the priest performs nearly all of the rituals by himself, the congregation's activity being pretty much confined to a few prayers and chants.

In point of fact, the struggle between the flesh and the spirit may be said to form the very axis of the teachings and practices of Orthodoxy. This struggle is rarely personalized, since its various dangers and triumphs are strictly worked out, as with Catholicism, according to a thorough and systematic ecclesiastical economy. In addition, the church's general attitude toward sexuality appears to be extremely negative and debilitating. Marriage and children seem to be the sole purposes of sexual relations, with enjoyment and tenderness hardly ever being factored in. Finally, not only has the concept of morality in general been reduced to the keeping of certain commandments, it has been strictly confined to the personal realm, conveniently excluding any implications for socio-political responsibility and activity. Despite such negative emphases, the Orthodox church, like many other religions traditions and communities, continues to be a major factor in the lives of millions of people. It would seem that some positive, deep human need continues to be met through such religious beliefs and practice, in spite of the many scholarly announcements that we have already entered the "post-Christian" era.

These specific considerations provide us with a convenient opportunity to direct this exploration of the "Classical heritage" back to Crete. I have, to be sure, been using this category in its broadest possible sense, while tracing out the twists and turns of the Greek approach to the relationship between body and mind. In many ways nearly all of the foregoing themes are reunited in the person and work of the great painter, El Greco. Kyriakos Theotokopoulos, the man we have come to call "El Greco," was born around 1547 in the tiny Cretan village of Fodele, just west of Iraklion. As a young man, he was trained as a painter in the style of the late Byzantine tradition, learning to do frescoes and mosaics. Early in his youth, however, he left for Italy, working as an artist in Venice and briefly visiting both Florence and Rome. By 1577 he had moved to Toledo, Spain, where he spent the remainder of his life, acquiring increasing fame as a painter and the name "El Greco."

El Greco is both interesting and important because in his aesthetic eclecticism he managed to bring together three quite distinct styles in his paintings. For, he combined, late Byzantine mysticism with high Renaissance realism and Spanish mannerism or baroque style. What is often overlooked, however, is that in this complex synthesis, El Greco also managed to integrate the Eastern Orthodox tradition with that of Western Roman Catholicism. While there is a certain "flatness: to his painted figures, reminiscent of Byzantine icons, there is also a great deal of the motion, curvature, and color characteristic of the Renaissance. For any number of reasons the Catholic tradition in Spain had resisted this active realism, but El Greco was able to combine it with an other-worldly feeling or tone that seems to merge his style with the content of his paintings. In this way he combined the mystical tradition of Orthodoxy with the down-to-earth character of Western Christianity.

On a more specific level, in the individual paintings of El Greco one can see his concern to treat the heavenly and the earthly realms as distinct yet inter-related. He follows the general conventions of placing the heavenly reality in the upper part of the painting, directing the gaze and posture of the earthly characters upward, and so forth. Such conventions tend to reinforce the traditional dualism of Medieval theology, inherited largely from Plato through Augustine. A distinctive feature of El Greco's work, however, is the flowing elongation of the bodies of his subjects. Perhaps one could say that this technique is meant to suggest the incarnation of spiritual reality in human forms of an earthly reality. Also, in many of his paintings of traditional religious scenes, the light source is within the scene, rather than coming from above or outside of it. This, too, serves to bring divine reality into the midst of human reality. Helen Gardner's Art Through the Ages epitomizes El Greco's style, in the following manner: "To make the inner meaning of his paintings forceful he developed a highly personal style in which his attenuated forms become etherealized in dynamic swirls of unearthly light and color. While there may be some ambiguity in El Greco's forms, there is none in his meaning, which is an expression of devout ecstatic mysticism and spirituality" (p. 575).

In any case, it is clear that El Greco, as a Cretan Greek, continued to wrestle with the relationship between body and mind, or spirit, in much the same way as his predecessors had from the Minoans and ancient Greeks right up through the Orthodox church. In my opinion he, like Aristotle, devised a far better, more integrative and holistic way of relating these two crucial dimensions of human experience than did Plato and Orthodoxy. Aristotle and El Greco's achievements stand in close proximity to the dynamic harmony created in Periclean Athens, and perhaps even to that of the Minoans of ancient Crete. Perhaps with the continual unearthing of more and more fragments of Linear A further light may be shed on the precise way in which the Minoans approached this entire issue. In the meantime, it surely is worth one's while to visit the little village in which El Greco was born and raised, and to contemplate the samples of his early work housed in the church there.

El Greco is the earliest of Crete's two most famous creative artists. The latest is the writer Nikos Kazantzakis. It is both interesting and fitting that his last work, which is largely autobiographical, is entitled Report to Greco. His other, more well-known works, several of which have been made into films, include Zorba The Greek, The Greek Passion, and The LastTemptation of Christ. In all of these books, Kazantzakis continues struggling with the relationship among the body, the mind, and the spirit, as well as endeavoring to establish Crete's place in world history and culture. Since my own introduction to Crete and all things Cretan came by means of my interest in Kazantzakis' work, it surely is appropriate that the final phase of these reflections be devoted to a brief examination of his life and thought. It will become evident in the following chapter that Kazantzakis also reflected on the Minoans, the "Golden Age" of Greece, and the teachings of Orthodoxy. Only a first-hand encounter with his works, however, will reveal the power, depth, and originality of his reflections.

When I first came to Greece, in 1966, I came for the same reason many other Americans and northern Europeans have come; I had read Nikos Kazantzakis' novel, Zorba the Greek. Although today the vast majority of sun-seekers coming to Crete have never heard of either the Minoans or Kazantzakis, there was a time when the latter's works were quite well-known. In fact, Zorba himself served as something of a patron saint for a great many spiritually "displaced persons" during the sixties and seventies. This accounts for the continued popularity of the film, at least on late night television, and the Broadway musical "Zorba The Greek," both starring Anthony Quinn. In recent years the film of Kazantzakis' novel, The Last Temptation of Christ, has created quite a stir in religious circles, being protested by Catholics and fundamentalists alike.

When I returned to Crete in 1972, spending my first summer in Mochlos, it was to write a book on Kazantzakis thought. After all, he was born, raised, and buried here; and in between he wrote about it incessantly. Although my manuscript never became a book, over the years I have continued to study and teach Kazantzakis' works, managing to publish a brief essay or two along the way. There also have been innumerable conversations with various friends on Crete about the meaning and influence of this most famous modern-day Greek writer. In addition, in 1972 it was my great pleasure and privilege to spend a whole day with Eleni Kazantzakis, Nikos' widow, when she was in exile in Geneva during the military dictatorship in Greece. She was as full of stories about Kazantzakis as she was of charm and insights of her own. In fact Eleni's biography of Kazantzakis, based on his letters, together with her tireless efforts to keep his works in print, are the chief reasons for whatever continued popularity he enjoys.

In this final chapter the aim will be to present the life and main themes of Kazantzakis' thought in relation to the various emphases of the previous chapters. In addition to the philosophical and religious dimensions of his highly creative works, there is as well throughout his life and books a continual returning to and reflecting on Crete throughout his life and books. Indeed, in one place he mentions carrying a jar of Cretan soil with him wherever

Kazantzakis Portrait Historical Museum Iraklion

he went in his extremely extensive travels, so that he could renew his spiritual strength through the contact with the land of his roots. Although the survey of Kazantzakis' life and thought provided in this chapter can in no way do justice to the magnitude of his creative genius, perhaps it will serve both as a capstone to my own tribute to Crete and as a stimulus to the reader to pursue a deeper, firsthand acquaintance with the works of this most powerful and insightful son of Crete.

Kazantzakis was born in Iraklion in 1883, amidst the violence of periodic Cretan rebellion against the oppressive Turkish 400 year occupation. After these revolutionary efforts were finally successful, he was free to study law at the University of Athens and do graduate work in Paris, where he studied both Henri Bergson and Friedrich Nietzsohe. After returning to Greece in 1909, he published and edited a great number of books and political essays in collaboration with his first wife Galatea, and served in several governmental administrative positions. Kazantzakis' frequent travels throughout Europe and post-revolutionary Russia greatly stimulated and broadened his views, causing him to incorporate various features of both Buddhism and Communism into his world view.

During the 1930's and the years of the Second World War, Kazantzakis lived with his second wife Eleni on the island of Aegina and wrote many of his most important novels. After the war, he resumed with his world-wide travel, minor political involvements,

Kazantzakis Funeral Historical Museum Iraklion

Kazantzakis Grave "I hope for nothing, I fear nothing, I'm free."

and multiple translation projects. During the early 1950's, although he was frequently ill, he became increasingly famous, having his many works published in a great number of languages and being nominated for the Nobel Prize in literature. Kazantzakis died in Freiburg in 1957. After being refused burial in Athens because of his unorthodox religious views, his body was interred in a prestigious spot atop the Venetian wall surrounding the old city of Iraklion. Thousands of Cretans attended the ceremony and

Kazantzakis writing disk

these words were inscribed on his gravestone: "I hope for nothing. I fear nothing. I am free."

One of the dominant concerns of Kazantzakis' life was the struggle to free and honor Crete. The character of the Cretan people has been formed in the crucible of oppression and revolution and Kazantzakis grew up in the midst of both. Throughout his life he felt the pressure of his father's prediction that his son would fail to honor Crete through "weak bottomed pen-pushing." Although Kazantzakis eventually resolved this conflict between political activism and abstract thought by viewing his literary efforts as a different, perhaps higher form of activism, he also felt a need to write a novel dealing with Crete's struggle for freedom. The book <u>Freedom or Death</u> traces the different dimensions of this struggle in the interaction amongst its various Cretan and Turkish characters and events in 1889. Each generation of Cretans rose up in revolt against their oppressors, and this is a story of one such uprising. It is no accident, by the way, that the main character, Captain Michalis, bears the same name as Kazantzakis' father.

Captain Michalis is a true "Palikari," a fierce mountain warrior of great courage and pride. His personal conflict with his Turkish counterpart, Nuri Bey, gradually escalates into a full-fledged rebellion of Crete against its oppressors. There are various subjects involving Captain Michalis' brother and the "politicians" of both sides who strive to keep the peace, as well as a number of grandfathers, cousins, and nephews. There is, as well, a beautiful woman, Emine, who becomes, like Crete, a major axis around which the plot develops. The long telling of the story, with its numerous characters and events, allows Kazantzakis to paint a vivid picture of the direct rugged quality of Cretan life, as well as of the honor and humor of the people, near the turn of the century. The sense of national and personal loyalty, coupled with a rigid and traditional moral code, serves both to motivate and to imprison all the characters alike.

The central image of this adventure is introduced near the middle of the book by means of a painting in which Crete is depicted as a woman on the cross of Christ wearing silver pistols and cartridges. In the minds and hearts of the revolutionaries, Crete has become a sacrifice to God in order to bring about its own resurrection of liberation from Turkish rule. This, is of course, means that the warriors of the present generation must be willing to offer themselves in death in exchange for victory and freedom. Freedom or death, or perhaps freedom <u>and</u> death, but in any case, freedom for some through the death of others. The crucial battle is lost to the Turks, partly because Captain Michalis leaves his post temporarily to protect Emine. Out of remorse, he vows to fight until death, even though it is now clear that there can be no victory.

In the final scenes, Captain Michalis and a few others are huddled among the rocks on the top of the mountain. His young nephew, Kosmos, who has been educated as a teacher in Europe and has just returned to Crete with his Jewish bride, seeks to join them in defeat and death. When Captain Michalis asks who sent him, Kosmos replies "Crete." But he is met with a reply: "None of your big words, schoolmaster! Talk like a man. And don't tell me Crete sends you! Do you hear? I am Crete." A bit later Kosmos is told to "clear out!" but he replies: "I'm not going!" He was transformed. A dark, unfathomable ecstasy possessed him. He felt light, and released, as if at this precise moment he had at last come home to his own country. He thought of nothing any more. All Frankish, intellectual ideas had vanished, together with mother, wife, and son. Nothing remained standing, except this single ancient duty. Freedom or death." Here we clearly see Kazantzakis seeking his own "salvation" through identification with his warrior father-image in the defense of Crete, even while fulfilling his calling as an artist by writing a novel about his historical event.

Later on in his career, Kazantzakis also wrote, in a book entitled <u>The Fratricides</u>, about the civil war which ravaged Greece after World War Two. Here, too, he depicts the fierce loyalty that Greeks in general feel for their country and national heritage, even to the point of killing their fellow countrymen in the name of honor and liberty. This fundamental rivalry, now transformed into the political mode, still divides the Greek people today, even though they continue to stand together against further Turkish aggression, as on Cyprus in 1974. On Crete this image of the warrior-hero, the "Palikari," remains especially strong, having been rekindled by the resistance movement against the Nazi occupation in the early 1940's. Yet the political stalemate between socialism and capitalism, which paralyzes Greek cultural life, continues to separate one Cretan farmer or merchant from another.

Recently I had conversation about such matters with two very thoughtful Cretan persons, one a policeman and the other a professor. Christos, the policeman, observed how strange it is that Cretan people can express warm genuine hospitality to strangers, while at the same time questioning and worrying whether or not these strangers have some ulterior motive for being in Crete. He said, "If you come to my home, my mother will feed you well and give you a place to sleep, but she will ask me what you are doing here, anyway." This suspicious attitude is rather like the backside of the Cretan pride that Kazantzakis writes about in Freedom or Death. In fact, this same Christos remarked that reading Kazantzakis made him feel so very proud of the land which produced such a great mind and talent.

Dimitri, the professor, not only traced this schizophrenic posture toward strangers to the hundreds of years of oppressive occupation by foreigners, but he saw within it a key to the division one sees in Greek society between the public and the private. Even after gaining independence one hundred and fifty years ago, Greece patterned its political structure after that of France, wherein nearly everything, continued to be decided and provided by the state officials. Dimitri hypothesized that this continued reliance on the determinations of the government has perpetuated an "us" versus "them" attitude in nearly all Greek people. This, in turn, largely takes away any sense of individual initiative for issues that do not directly concern the individual or the family. "Thus," he said, "almost every private home is kept immaculately clean, but public roads and undeveloped areas are littered with trash and junk."

The overall point here is that there may be a direct, though inverse, connection between government from above and the lack of initiative and responsibility at the public level. This is undoubtedly intensified if those in charge favor themselves and their rich friends. This division between the private and the public, especially under foreign and oppressive occupation, heads inevitably to a deep suspicion, not only toward strangers, but toward one's neighbors as well. On Crete, it is safe to say, where independence is less than one hundred years old and political decisions are made 150 miles away in mainland Athens, deep pride and strong suspicion continue to thrive side by side. Kazantzakis' Freedom or Death captures the essence of this dimension of the reality that is Crete.

Because of Martin Scorcese's film based on it, <u>The Last Temptation of Christ</u> is currently the most well-known of Kazantzakis' novels. In this book he attempts to portray the inner struggle that must have taken place in Jesus' heart and mind between his inherent humanity and his growing Messianic consciousness. He does this by putting flesh and blood on the characters and events for which the Gospel accounts in the New Testament provide the barest skeleton. The personages of Peter, Mary Magdalene, and Judas, for instance, are imaginatively yet believably developed in the context of Jesus' story. Jesus himself is depicted as a tormented young carpenter who becomes convinced against his will that he is God's special servant, and who convinces politically minded Judas to betray him in order to trigger the apocalypse.

Along the way to his predetermined end, Jesus agonizes with his mother and his somewhat reluctant apostles over the meaning of love in relation to the military oppression of the Jews by the Roman Empire. He gains insight and peace from a crucial visit in a desert monastery, and struggles with his sexual attraction to Mary Magdalene. He also suffers from guilt for having withdrawn from their relationship because of his "calling," driving her thereby to a life of prostitution. This realistic, humanistic portrayal of Jesus caused the Pope to place <u>The Last Temptation</u> on the Catholic Index of books not to be read by Catholics, and nearly resulted in Kazantzakis being excommunicated by the Greek Orthodox Church. A few years ago the film based on the novel drew a similar reaction, being banned by default and boycotted by defenders of the faith" world-wide.

Kazantzakis himself was dismayed and hurt by such reactions. In his Prologue to the book he says that he wrote the novel in order to offer a supreme model to those who suffer from temptation, pain, and death, "because all three can be conquered, all three have already been conquered" in Christ. Moreover, he expressed confidence that every open minded person who reads this book, "so filled as it is with love, will more than ever before, better than ever before, love Christ." It must be admitted, however, that Kazantzakis' interpretation of the person and theological significance of Jesus Christ is at best unorthodox. Quite apart from the trivial question of his natural sexual desires and the nontrivial issue of whether or not he was resurrected, there remains a decided schizophrenic quality to Kazantzakis' Jesus that seems a bit overdrawn.

The marked conflict between his own desires and those foisted upon him by what he takes to be God render this imaginative Jesus as one possessed. Even his crucial message of "love one another" comes into and out of his mouth without passing through his mind, as if from delivered by means of a medium in a trance. In the opening lines of his Prologue, Kazantzakis admits that "the dual substance of Christ," the human urge to unite with God and to become superhuman," has always been a deep inscrutable mystery" to him. "My principle anguish and the source of all my joys and sorrows from my youth onward has been the incessant, merciless battle between the spirit and the flesh." The dualism inherent within such statements take us back to the central theme of the previous chapter.

It will be recalled that one important issue around which the developments comprising the Classical heritage revolved was the relation between the mind and the body. It can be said, in fact, that the dynamic balance achieved between these two crucial dimensions of human existence by the "Golden Age," and perhaps even by the earlier Minoans, was undermined by the pervasive influence of Plato's basic division between them. This radical dualism between body and mind, or spirit, has carried right on down through the faith and practice of both Medieval and modern Orthodox theology. Indeed, it constitutes the fundamental intellectual and affective inheritance so clearly evidenced throughout Kazantzakis' works and so succinctly focused in the words of quoted above. In embracing this dichotomy between "spirit and flesh," Kazantzakis buys into all the theological and philosophical dilemm as which have plagued Western thought ever since Plato.

The agonizing force of this Western dualism is very clearly embodied in the climactic chapters of <u>The Last Temptation of Christ</u>. In Kazantzakis own words, when Jesus was finally placed upon the cross: But even there his struggle did not end-Temptation the Last Temptation-was waiting for him upon the Cross. Before the fainted eyes of the Crucified the spirit of the Evil One, in an instantaneous flash, unfolded the deceptive vision of a calm and happy life. It seemed to Christ that he had taken the smooth, easy road of men. He had married and fathered children. People loved and respected him. Now, an old man, he sat on the threshold of his house and smiled with satisfaction as he recalled the longings of his youth. How splendidly, how sensibly he had acted in choosing the road of men! What insanity to have wanted to save the world! What joy to have escaped the privations, the tortures, and the Cross! But Jesus awoke from this dream to discover that he had not succumbed to this final temptation, that he had remained true to the calling of God, had chosen the way of the spirit over the way of the flesh.

What is evident here is that in Kazantzakis' view, as well as in the traditional Western understanding, these two central and powerful aspects of human existence are essentially opposed and mutually exclusive. What is offered to Jesus, as well as to the rest of us, is the hard choice between the human and the divine. Choose one or the other, but it is impossible to have both. Kazantzakis frequently characterizes his solution to this dilemma as the "transubstantiation of flesh into spirit." This goes along quite well with the traditional Christian doctrine of the immortality of the soul, wherein it is claimed that we shall leave our moral bodies and ascend into the spiritual presence of the divine.

In my own view, there are at least three major difficulties with this traditional interpretation, accepted in principle even by Kazantzakis. To begin with, the New Testament, along with the Apostle's Creed, makes it quite clear that human souls are not immortal. The fundamental Christian hope is for the resurrection of the body, not the immortality of the soul. The belief in the soul's eternal character derives from Plato, not the Bible. Even Jesus is said to have really died prior to having been resurrected. Thus Christians, unlike Platonists, look forward to a "new Heaven and a new Earth" in resurrected albeit "spiritual bodies," not to an eternal, disembodied existence. Kazantzakis' Jesus turns out not to be so unorthodox as he first appears to be, since he is portrayed as caught within this traditional, though unbiblical dualism.

Secondly, Christ's struggle between the spirit and the flesh, along with his choice of the former over the latter, as presented by Kazantzakis, flies in the face of the simple fact that nowhere in the New Testament is there any indication of Jesus having anything like a "split-personality." There are no passages in the Gospel accounts of Jesus engaged in a struggle between two natures, one divine and the other human. He is consistently depicted as a fully integrated person. The "two natures" idea does not arise until the early church fathers gathered together to try and explain the notion of incarnation in theoretical terms. Even in the scene in the Garden of Gethsemane, where Jesus says "Nevertheless, not my will but Thine," the contrast is not between two natures in the same person, but between two alternatives confronting one, unified person.

In his effort to overcome what might be called the "Clark Kent" view of Jesus, Kazantzakis over-shot the mark. While too many Christians think of Christ as a kind of superman disguised as a "mild-mannered carpenter from Nazareth," Kazantzakis portrays him as a person divided against himself at the most fundamental level. Both ignore the actual gospel records. Whatever else can be said about the Jesus of the New Testament, it is perfectly clear that his life was neither one which knew no real temptations, nor one which pitted the divine against the human. His primary concern was to enable others to accept and live according to the radical nature of divine reconciling love.

Thirdly, the implications of Kazantzakis' formula for spiritual achievement, both for Christ and for the rest of us, as the "transubstantiation of flesh into spirit" runs directly contrary to the central thrust of the Christian idea of incarnation. The biblical teaching is that in Jesus "the Word became flesh and dwelt among us." Even though this pronouncement expresses the resultant faith of the early Christians, rather than a direct announcement from God, the point is clear that rather than Christ representing a transcendence of human flesh, he is to be understood as the enfleshment of the divine spirit. For Christ, as well as for others, the path of God consists in transubstantiating spirit into flesh, rather than the other way around. So, Kazantzakis' portrayal of the last temptation as an acceptance of a "normal life," instead of one of suffering for others on God's behalf, is overly simplistic. These two alternatives do not exhaust the possibilities. Surely one can seek to know and do the will of God without becoming a Martyr.

Kazantzakis wrote two other novels in which a similar but just as one-sided is presented. One, The Greek Passion which was made into an excellent film entitled "He Who Must Die," tells the story of a small Greek village which sets about to re-enact Christ's passion and death. The villagers are given their assigned parts a whole year in advance, and the story tells of the character transformations during the ensuing year. Of course, the novel revolves around the young man who is to play Christ, who is not accidentally named Manolios, which is short for Immanuel. In the process of growing into his role, Manolios gradually renounces every aspect of normal human existence, and in the end he dies giving his life for others. Once more we encounter Kazantzakis' fundamental dualism between body and mind or flesh and spirit.

The other novel where this theme is reiterated is <u>Saint Frances</u>, which provided Kazantzakis an opportunity to eulogize one of his favorite historical characters. Here again we see a person dramatizing the decision to follow God's path in terms of the dilemma between a normal human life and one of total self-sacrifice. It is well-known that Saint Frances renounced all of his father's riches and dedicated his life to helping others. At one point Kazantzakis even has him determine what God would have him do next by asking himself what he would most loath doing. The answer, obviously, is to hug, kiss, and care for lepers, so he runs to find some lepers and begins a colony for them. Even if such stories are only meant to function as graphic symbols, the choices they offer are exceedingly misleading.

Not only are there more options and nuances involved in life than simply choosing between being a Mother Theresa or failing in the eyes of God, but this type of forced-option makes it far too easy to get oneself off the hook, spiritually speaking, by merely acknowledging that one is not a saint. The downside of having such shining examples as Saint Frances and Mother Theresa is that we ourselves become morally paralyzed by their greatness. We end up saying to ourselves something like, "Well, I could never be like that, so I guess that lets me out." It's just too easy to forget that Frances and Theresa were not "saints" either when they started out. As Gertrude Stein might put it, "A saint is a saint is a saint."

This same question of the relationship between mind, spirit, and body forms the axis around which everything revolves in what may well be Kazantzakis' most well-known, if not greatest novel, <u>Zorba the Greek</u>. The story begins with "The Boss," who for the most part represents Kazantzakis himself, meeting and hiring a simple workman named Alexis Zorbas to help him mine lignite on

Crete. The Boss is a highly educated and refined writer and Zorba turns out to be an extremely wise, experienced, and spontaneous character who works, dances, and makes love to women with equal abandon. So well-known, indeed, has Kazantzakis' Zorba become, it is actually tempting to describe the character in the novel as a regular Zorba! Right at the outset we discover that the Boss who orders tea, is all boxed-in by his rationality and conventionality, while Zorba, who orders rum, listens only to the dictates of his body and his feelings.

Although the duality between flesh and spirit does enter into the dynamics of the story by way of the Boss' enamorement of Buddhism, the basic drama is that between the Boss, with his books and ideas, on the one hand, Zorb†, with his emotions and deeds, on the other hand. Throughout the book the Boss is continually challenged by Zorbas robust actions and accused by his unanswerable questions about the meaning of life, death, love, and war. He finds himself wishing desperately that he could be more like Zorba.

> *My life is wasted, I thought. If only I could take a cloth and wipe out all I have learnt, all I have seen and heard, and go to Zorba's school and start the great, the real alphabet! What a different road I would choose. I should keep my five senses perfectly trained, and my whole body, too, so that it would enjoy and understand. I should learn to run, to wrestle, to swim, to ride horses, to row, to drive a car, to fire a rifle. I should fill my soul with flesh. I should fill my flesh with soul. In fact, I should reconcile at last within me the two eternal antagonists.*

Now what is fascinating about the way the relation between mind and body is approached in this book is that it seems just the reverse of that taken in the books discussed on the foregoing pages. Rather than advocating a movement away from the body toward the mind, or the spirit, Zorba The Greek urges us to work ourselves free from the limitations imposed by abstract though so as to live life more directly and fully through the body. Basically the same dualism seems to be present in this Kazantzakis novel, the mind and the body pitted against each other, but now the vector is clearly running in the opposite direction. In short, although he has here returned to the issues posed by Plato, Kazantzakis is busy turning Plato upside down, much as Marx claimed to be standing Hegel on his head.

There are three constrastive sub-themes running through <u>Zorba the Greek</u> which clearly demonstrate the central thrust of Kazantzakis' creative energy at this juncture. The first has to do with the contrast between the Boss' manuscript and Zorba's mine. The former, a manuscript dealing with the philosophy of Buddhism, serves as a symbol of the Boss' overly intellectual concern with an ephemeral realm. He works sporadically at completing this manuscript throughout the novel, until he finally discards it as a sign of his enrollment in "Zorba's School." Zorba, meanwhile, works away in the lignite mine, cursing the men who work under him, discovering new vanes, and designing a contraption with which to bring timber down from the mountainside for supporting the ceilings of the mine shafts. In the end, his scheme collapses, symbolizing the inadequacy and expendability of technology and rationalistic planning.

The second such sub-theme pertains to the two men's attitudes toward women. Zorba throws himself into romantic and sexual activity with great seriousness and abandon, focusing in this instance on the widow, Madam Hortense. The Boss, on the other hand, is not only extremely conventional and overly shy in relation to women, but is strongly inhibited by a deep fear of anything physical. For a long time he resists the urging of his own body, as well as those of Zorba, to approach a beautiful young widow in the village where they are staying. At last, however, he conquers his inhibitions and lets himself experience the joys of sexual union advancing to the next level in "Zorba's School." Toward the end of the novel, both Madam Hortense and the young widow die ignominious deaths, signifying their essentially secondary role in the lives of the two male characters. We shall return to this issue of the nature of male and female relationships in Kazantzakis' works a bit latter on.

The third contrast between the Boss and Zorba is that between their modes of physical expression. Basically, the Boss talks with his mouth, as an extension of his brain, and Zorba chastises him for never using his hands, arms, and chest when he speaks. Zorba, on the other hand, can only really express himself well by playing his santuri or by dancing. In their last scene together, at the Boss' request, Zorba begins to teach him to dance, thereby advancing yet another level in "Zorba's School." The turning point for the Boss in his struggle to transcend, or "subscend," the entrapments of his intellectualist way of life, comes one day while out for a walk. He realizes that his body has made a simple decision for him as to which path to take. Later, at the seashore, he receives his "baptism" into Zorba's naturalistic religion.

> I looked about me. It was quite dark. The last of the villagers had gone, no one could see me, I was absolutely alone. I bared my feet and dipped them in the sea. I rolled on the sand. I felt an urge to touch the stones, the water, and the air with my bare body. The Mother Superior had exasperated me with her "eternity," and I felt the word fall about me, like a lasso catching a wild horse. I made a leap to try to escape. I felt a desire to press my naked body against the earth and the sea, to feel with certainty that these beloved ephemeral things really exited.
> "You exist, and you alone!" I cried in my innermost self. "O Earth! I am you last-born, I am sucking at your breast and will not let go. You do not let me live for more than one minute, but that minute turns into a breast and I such" (p.174).

It is difficult to gage the overall significance of this forthright contrast between the mind and the body in Kazantzakis' life and thought. For one thing, his encounter with the real-life Zorba came rather early in his adult life, when he was still struggling with the guilt imposed by his father over his choice of an intellectual career. In addition, not only is it possible to explore the possibility that Zorba actually learns some things from the Boss, but it may be that the novel is actually a creative device for setting up the traditional dualism between mind and body. Kazantzakis may actually be recommending a synthesis of the two ways of life, since it should be evident that neither the Boss nor Zorba is a complete person without the other. To be sure, each person must find their own peculiar balance of these contrasting, but equally essential dimensions of life in achieving Aristotle's "Golden Mean." It is clear that Kazantzakis came to feel his balance was to be found in the life of a creative writer, that artistic formulation is itself a legitimate form of activity.

For my own part, it is necessary to acknowledge my deep indebtedness to Kazantzakis' Zorba for providing a vision of the importance of integrating the physical and mental dimensions of human existence. My own particular embodiment of these two symbiotic aspects of life is, on the one hand, much more physical than was that of Kazantzakis', since athletic activity and sculpting in stone have been fully and continuously incorporated into it. On the other hand, it is perfectly clear as well that whatever Kazantzakis may have lacked in terms of the somatic dimension, he more than compensated for with the superb quality of his literary and theoretic achievement. In any case, the point is made that a full and growing human life must include, in an <u>integral</u> manner both physical and mental activity. Moreover, at least in my view this integration necessarily involves more than thinking and doing on merely a practical or "hobby" level, though these are not thereby excluded. The Classical ideal of the complete and balanced integration of intellectual and physical excellence remains both viable and supremely worthy.

The question of the degree to which Kazantzakis was able to combine the intellectual and artistic with physical and political activity immediately involves us in the broader issue of the overall development of his life and thought. He recounts the steps of this development in <u>Report to Greco</u>. In addition to wrestling with the disappointment of his father and the narrow structures of the Orthodox church, Kazantzakis was continuously engaged in absorbing and evaluating his Cretan and Greek heritage. On the other hand, he was quite taken with the character and accomplishments of the Minoans. It must be borne in mind that Kazantzakis was just leaving Crete to study at the University of Athens when Arthur Evans began excavating Knossos in 1900. Upon graduating, he returned to spend the summer with his family and gather strength from the Cretan soil. His encounter with Knossos led him to write the following words:

> Crete's mystery is extremely deep. Whoever sets foot on this island senses a mysterious force branching warmly and beneficently through his veins, senses his soul begin to grow. But this mystery has become even deeper and richer since the discovery of this immensely versatile and

*varicolored civilization until then buried beneath the soil,
this civilization filled with such great nobility and youthful
joy* (p. 147).

While at Knossos, Kazantzakis met an old woman who gave him two figs, and when he asked why she said this, she replied quite simply: "You're a human being, aren't you" So am I. Isn't that enough?" He also had a discussion with a French Catholic priest about why the latter had bowed in prayer before the Minaon image of the double-edged axe. The priest answered: "Every race and every age gives God its own mask. But behind all the masks...is always the same never changing God...I push aside the ephemeral symbols and discern the same God behind both the cross and the double-edged axe." These two brief exchanges at Knossos not only strongly flavored Kazantzakis' appreciation for and under standing of the ancient Minoans, but they deeply influenced his overall philosophy of life and religion, as well. We shall return to this latter topic shortly.

When he first arrived in Athens to begin his studies, Kazantzakis was confronted by the Parthenon, the single most impressive symbol of his classical heritage. Somehow, after so many years of expectation, the Parthenon did not impress Kazantzakis; it just stood there, inert. Later he wrote that "Throughout my life this has served me as an infallible sign. When I encounter a sunrise, a painting, a woman, or an idea that makes my heart bound like a young calf, then I know I am standing in front of happiness. The first time I stood in front of the Parthenon, my heart did not bound" (p. 136). At this point in his life, this great monument was "too much like an even number to touch the human heart." Slowly, however, his appreciation for the Parthenon and all that it stands for grew, and finally he did feel his heart bound like a young calf. Here is how he describes his new found appreciation:

*This temple that towered before me, what a trophy it was, what
a collaboration between mind and heart, what a supreme fruit
of human effort! Space had been conquered; distinctions between
small and large had vanished. Infinity entered this narrow, magical
parallelogram carved out by man, entered leisurely and took
its repose there. Time had been conquered as well; the lofty
moment had been transformed into eternity* (p. 137).

The two major struggles of Kazantzakis' adult life were with Communism and women. We shall consider them one at a time. As was mentioned earlier, Kazantzakis was initially extremely taken by Lenin's vision of its early implementation in Russia. He saw in this revolution a chance for humankind to come together and rise above the petty wars and hierarchical political systems which had divided and decimated nearly all peoples down through history. In his visits to Russia, which were several and extensive, Kazantzakis met many people, peasants and famous folks alike, and he genuinely came to believe that this was a giant leap forward for all human beings. At the same time, his letters to his wife Galatea make it clear that he was equally aware of the obstacles which lay in the path of such a revolutionary experiment. Nevertheless, he spent a number of years endeavoring to educate and motivate people in Greece and Crete concerning Communist ideology.

Gradually, however, Kazantzakis began to feel a tension arising within him between socio-political involvement and the creative process. To put it bluntly, there are just so many hours in a day and any given person only has so much energy and talent; how can one be both active and comteplative, both political and artistic? This became the fundamental dilemma of Kazantzakis' life. If ·he continued to write, he felt guilty for not working to help humankind overcome poverty and oppression. If he stopped writing, even if only to dive into the world of political action, he felt guilty for not fulfilling his inner drive to comprehend in literary creations the meaning of the cosmos. Eventually, he and Galatea drifted apart as a result of his inability to make a full commitment to Communist praxis. Even meeting Zorba only exacerbated his agony. Many years of his life were spent dividing his time between political activity, world travel, and various kinds of journalism.

In was, in fact, the news of Zorba's death in 1942, that served as the catalyst for Kazantzakis' personal resolution of the dilemma which had been haunting. At age fifty-eight, having already worked on the hard skeleton of his overall philosophy in his small book Saviors of God, (1923) and his huge epic poem The Odyssey: A Modern Sequel (1927), he was at loose-ends concerning the proper direction for his future when he learned of Zorba's death. At first he felt paralyzed by grief and anger, but then he saw that the way to counteract Zorba's death was to resurrect him in literary form. This was the turning point, although seemingly belated, for Kazantzakis' career as a novelist. Over the next ten years he wrote five more novels and reworked several of his previous efforts. In his own words, "The germ of 'The Odyssey' had finally begun to form fruit in his life." He spent his final years enfleshing his original ideas about life, death, love, and God in the various characters and events of his novels.

In essence Kazantzakis finally decided that being engaged in the creative process is itself a legitimate form of human <u>action</u>. He no longer felt forced to choose between a life of public responsibility and literary creation, for the latter is every bit as important as, though different from, the former. He could finally put the guilt he felt in relation to this father, Galatea, Lenin, and Zorba behind him, because he had found a way to educate and motivate people to a higher, richer life through his literary efforts. He had not, after all, disgraced Crete!

The second major struggle of Kazantzakis' adult life was with women-or better, with woman. In between his two marriages, he met a number of women while travelling in Europe, the two or three significant ones being Jewish and/or Russian. From his own account, these relationships were both stormy and productive of growth in his inner life. In his marriage to Eleni which lasted from 1930 until his death in 1957, Kazantzakis was supremely happy. The day I spent visiting Eleni in Geneva, she not only explained that she had met and become friends with Kazantzakis' previous women friends, but she took great delight in reminiscing about the richness of their marriage, in the face of many difficulties. I recall her remarking about Nikos' timely sense of humor and his ability to step down to the corner to buy a newspaper and return with five stories which he collected along the way.

When he writes autobiographically in his report to his Cretan "grandfather," El Greco, Kazantzakis acknowledges that "No man ever did me so much good or aided my struggle so greatly as the women I loved-and one above all, the last." At the same time, however, he goes on to stress that neither he nor El Greco allowed "women, even the dearest, to lead us astray." For him the struggle to ascend toward the ultimate in human potential to "reach what you cannot" is fundamentally an individual quest. Moreover, he reminds El Greco that their women "followed our ascents of their own free will," thereby suggesting that it is really only men, after all, who participate in the journey toward self-actualization. The simple fact is, whether because of traditional Greek enculturation or his own personality, or both, for Kazantzakis women are second-class citizens, existentially speaking.

This male chauvinism manifests itself quite clearly in Kazantzakis' novels where the women are either faithful wives and mothers useful entertainment, or temptations which lure men from their higher goals. Although this characterization of women as functionally necessary but ultimately dispensable pervades all of the novels mentioned previously, it is most evident in Zorba The Greek. Not only do the two women in this story play ancillary roles, but Zorba consistently talks of women in either dehumanizing or patronizing tones. On the one hand he says that women exist for only one purpose, since "all men who see her must desire her. That's what she wants, the poor creature, so you might try and please her." On the other hand, he claims that "Woman is something different, Boss...she's not human...Woman's something incomprehensible." The simple fact is, after all, that women are not really taken seriously as free and equal agents in either the Zorbatic world or the Kazantzakian world view.

Although it is possible to get Kazantzakis part of the way off this chauvinistic hook by taking note of the time and place of his upbringing, and by engaging in some creative interpretive efforts, little is really accomplished thereby. It seems more helpful to me simply to admit the unfortunate nature of this one-sidedness on his part and seek to broaden the scope of his deep and forceful insights concerning human existence to include women as well as men. In this way it becomes both possible and valuable to speak of female Zorbas as well as of male. Self-actualization of human potential is a viable goal for each and every person, and Kazantzakis' contribution to this dynamic need not and should not be lost sight of simply because he himself, as well as his traditional culture, failed to acknowledge the full personhood of women.

All of this brings us, finally, to a consideration of the exact nature of the Kazantzakian quest, this search in which one reaches for that which in principle is unattainable. This consideration will, in turn, involve us in an exploration of Kazantzakis' philosophy of religion and his view of God. Actually, he had these matters fairly well worked out in his own mind by the time he was forty years old, and he set them forth in his The Saviors of God and They Odyssey: A Modern Sequel. The former work provides a dense and conceptual summary of his overall philosophy, while the latter expands this summary into epic proportions poetically expressed. Kazantzakis' main novels, written some twenty to thirty years later, provide yet another literary incarnation of his world view and personal vision.

In his Prologue to The Saviors of God, Kazantzakis stresses the undeniability of two conflicting forces within all that exists, the force toward death. Neither can be negated, nor can either be affirmed unilaterally. He concludes that: "It is out duty, therefore, to grasp that vision which can embrace and harmonize these two enormous, timeless, and indestructible forces, and with this vision to modulate our thinking and our action" (p. 44). Here we see the influence of both of Kazantzakis' philosophical mentors, Henri Bergson and Friedrich Nietzsche. Both saw the two forces as providing the dynamic of evolutionary development, Bergson on the cultural level and Nietzsche on the personal level. In "The Preparation," Kazantzakis sets down three duties: 1. "to see and accept the boundaries of the human mind without vain rebellion" and to work within them, 2. to deny these mental boundaries by following the urgings of one's heart for the reality behind the appearances, and 3. to transcend the hopes and fears of the heart by choosing to be free from them, to accept the fact that life and death are ultimately meaningless.

This latter emphasis places Kazantzakis squarely within the existentialist movement, which takes its impetus largely from Nietzsche. As Camus, a French contemporary of Kazantzakis put it, in order to be a truly authentic and free human being, it is necessary to "accept the benign indifference of the universe." Only when we have ceased both to hope and to fear, in both life and death, can we be liberated from the rewards and threats which enslave us. Only then, according to Kazantzakis, can we be "saved from salvation." This is why he requested that the following words be carved on his headstone: "I hope for nothing, I fear nothing, I am free." This was Kazantzakis' credo, both in death and, more importantly, in life. It was this freedom toward which the Boss strove and which Zorba embodied. According to Zorba, such freedom only comes from cutting the string that ties one to the mundane cares of everyday life. It takes "a touch of folly" to be able to cut this string, and this is what Zorba had that the Boss lacked. To be authentic, one must be willing to risk everything

In his section of The Saviors of God entitled "The March," Kazantzakis suggests that what calls us forth toward itself is God; not the traditional god of any established religion, but the surging energy of the Cosmos. He labels this cosmic energy the "Cry" of the future that is within each ego, each race, all of humanity and even in the earth itself. This evolving Spirit or life force seeks to actualize and fulfill itself by surging through all matter and mind in an ever upward ascent, transforming all that is flesh into pure Spirit. In the section labeled "The Vision" Kazantzakis focuses this primordial process in this way:

> Which is that one force amid all of God's forces which man is able to grasp? Only this: We discern a crimson line on this earth, a red, blood-splattered line which ascends, struggling, from matter to plants, from plants to animals, from animals to man.
> This indestructible prehuman rhythm is the only visible journey of the Invisible on this earth. Plants, animals, and men are the steps which God creates on which to tread and to mount upward.
> Difficult, dreadful, unending ascension! Shall God conquer or be conquered in this onslaught? Does victory exist? Does defeat exist?

In Kazantzakis' view, God is not an omnipotent, omniscient Creator who sits transcendently above the world. Rather, God is the very force by means of which the cosmos struggles to realize its one spiritual nature, the life-principle rising up from prime matter through all biological, zoological, and human existence. Kazantzakis suggests that this cosmic evolutionary process has now reached the stage wherein its future depends, not upon further physical modification, but upon the transformation of minds and spirits into a yet higher, more spiritual form of life. And this final step in this process depends very much on our own full participation in it, since we are now conscious of the reality of the process itself. Kazantzakis puts it thusly:

*God is imperiled. He is not almighty, that we may cross
our hands, waiting for certain victory. He is not all-holy,
that we may wait trustingly for him to pity and to save us.
Within the province of our ephemeral flesh all of God is
imperiled. He cannot be saved unless we save him with
our own struggles; nor can we be saved unless he is saved*
(p. 105).

The ultimate goal of all of life, in both the cosmic and the personal
sense, is, according to Kazantzakis, growth itself. The primary
energy of nature strives to transform itself into ever higher forms
of life, and each individual must seek to do likewise. This is why
Kazantzakis chose Odysseus as the crucial image of human
existence, for this intrepid traveller, especially in Kazantzakis
modern sequel, refuses to become comfortable in any port. In his
Introduction to this great epic poem, Kimon Friar quotes
Kazantzakis:

*"Odysseus," he once said in a newspaper interview, "is
the man who has freed himself from everything-religious,
philosophies, political systems-one who has cut away
all the strings. He wants to try all the forms of life, freely,
beyond plans
and systems, keeping the thought of death before him as
a stimulant, not to make every pleasure more acrid or every
ephemeral moment more sharply enjoyable in its brevity,
but to whet his appetites in life, to make them more capable
of embracing and of exhausting all thins so that, when
death finally came, it would find nothing to take from him,
for it would find an entirely squandered Odysseus"* (p. xi).

As was mentioned earlier on, I myself have been strongly
influenced by this image of struggle and growth as the essence
and chief value of life. In addition, Kazantzakis' religious
"naturalism," which is not to be confused with "pantheism," strikes
me as a helpful way to avoid many of the dualistic difficulties
inherent within traditional the istic views. As I see it, following
Kazantzakis, God is neither to be identified with the cosmos, as
in pantheism, nor thought of as entirely independent of it, as in
traditional theism. Rather, God is to be understood as that centered

energy within the cosmos that strives to create an ever-higher mode of existence through love, beauty, and justice. Such a view, which has been refereed to as "panentheism," is essentially compatible with that of Alfred North Whitehead, as developed in his extremely important book, <u>Process and Reality</u>. However, there are two chief difficulties that I have with Kazantzakis' philosophy.

The first difficulty, as I remarked previously, concerns his characterization of this cosmic creative process as "the transubstantiation of flesh into spirit." It seems to me that this way of speaking locks one into the debilitating dualism of traditional Western thought. I not only think it more helpful to transpose this formula, so as to read "the transubstantiation of spirit into flesh," but I think this reading is actually more in line with the major thrust of Kazantzakis' overall philosophy. The point is not to get <u>beyond</u> material existence to some etherial state, but to incarnate spiritual reality into the very center of human life. This way of putting the matter also harmonizes more readily with central Christian idea of incarnation, "The Word became flesh."

My second difficulty with Kazantzakis' world view pertains to its excessive individualism. As is abundantly clear from the various discussions throughout this chapter, each character in Kazantzakis' novels, as well as in his own personal life, must strive for his or her own self-actualization as a solitary individual. Other persons may be of some help along the way, but our struggle upward must in the end be our own. In his <u>Report to Greco</u>, Kazantzakis even portrays his own creation, Odysseus, as leaving him behind like a used lemon rind. He has Odysseus say: "Who was the ascetic who sought God for forty years and could not find him? Some dark object loomed in the middle, hindering him. But one morning he saw: it was an old fur which he loved dearly and did not have the heart to discard. He threw it away, and all at once he saw God in front of him...You, dear companion, are my old fur. Farewell!" (p.492).

Not only is this sort of "atomism" out of line with the inter-connecting character of Whitehead's "process philosophy" mentioned above, but it goes hand in hand with the sort of dualism which has plagued Western thought since Plato's time. As we have been discovering in recent years, it is necessary to understand the evolutionary process, whether as physical or as spiritual, in terms of inter-active, ecological relationships which are mutually interdependent. Selfhood, too, must be seen as a function of inter-related, symbiotic processes, rather than as an individualistic reality. After all, inter-personal and socio-political relations are the warp and weft out of which the fabric of human existence is woven. Even the river and the river bed mutually define each other.

It is, indeed, possible to argue that in his actual practice, both in his life and in his work, Kazantzakis obviated the individualism he advocates in his theory. Not only did he form many mutually sustaining relationships throughout his life, but the individual characters in his creative writings derive their being, for good or ill, from their reciprocal interactions with one another. Moreover, in his most autobiographical work, <u>Report To Greece</u>, Kazantzakis sees his own life as patterned by his ancestors, the island of Crete, his travels, the ideas of his intellectual mentors, and most especially his many close friends and his wife Eleni. Indeed, at the close of his life he felt constrained to render an account of his own struggle to Crete's other internationally recognized creative artist, El Greco.

At the close of this final report, Kazantzakis dreams that El Greco confronts him with a choice between three kinds of prayers: 1. "I am a bow in your hands, Lord. Draw me lestI rot," 2. "Do not overdraw me, Lord. I shall break," 3. "Overdraw me, and who cares if I break." He responds to this challenge with these words:

"I chose. Now the twilight casts its haze upon the hilltops. The shadows have lengthened, the air has filled with the dead. The battle is drawing to a close. Did I win or lose? The only thing I know is this: I am full of wounds and still standing on my feet" (p. 512).

In other words, "Reach what you cannot!"

Conclusion

Admittedly, the six chapters comprising this short book, represent something of a hodgepodge. Specifically, the first three chapters, consist of mostly memories of my experiences on and around Crete, while the second three present my reflections on various realities emanating from the history and culture of this magical island. There are, however, certain themes which hopefully serve to bind them together. By way of bringing these memories and reflections to a conclusion, let me indicate four such themes that strike me as perhaps the more significant.

First, there is the land, a matter of geographical and geological place. The location and landscape of Crete, both in itself and in relation to mainland Greece, has served as the axis around which these memories and reflections have revolved. There is a unique "sense of place" associated with an island existence. Both privacy and self-reliance, on the one hand, and isolation and suspicion, on the other. Also, the mountainous terrain of Crete, as well as of mainland Greece, contributes to the character of one's experience there. This is attested to, not only in my own case, but in the history and culture of the Minoans and the classical Greeks, as well as in the life and thought of Nikos Kazantzakis. The contours of one's homeland, even if it is only an adopted homeland, deeply influence the shape and bent of one's character.

A second theme running through these chapters has been that of people. In a sense this book is simply an account of the many and various personal relationships that have enriched my life because of my adventures in Crete and Greece. From the people of Mochlos and Sitia, through the artistic and intellectual contributions of the Minoans and the ancient Greeks, down to the insights and energy of Kazantazakis, there has been a continual dialogue and interaction between myself and those persons who have made Crete and Greece what they are. Though I have not always been able to agree with those whom I have encountered, I am confident that the give and take of ideas and energy which has continuously transpired between myself and various Greek folk have greatly contributed to my own personal and intellectual growth. I can only hope that the same has been true for them. This on-going dialogue actually includes the evolving cultural and historical interaction amongst Minoan political leaders and artists on the one hand, and those of classical Greece, on the other hand. Hopefully, too, it will continue to engage the contemporary and coming generations of Cretans and Greeks.

A third theme uniting the foregoing chapters is that of <u>ideas</u>. Throughout my years of visiting and living on Crete, there has been a continual ideational conversation taking place in my own mind about the nature and meaning of village life, the significance of Minoan and Greek culture, and the implications of the thought of Plato, Aristotle, and Kazantzakis. Surely another person, who was not a thinker by training and vocation, would have experienced all of the phenomena introduced in this book quite differently. That is as it should be. For this person, however, it has been both necessary and profitable to interact with the conceptual dimension of those persons, things, and events that I have encountered. Moreover, in my own view, every person's experience is both better understood and enhanced by a significant amount of reflective activity. One can, indeed, think about things too much, but one can just as easily, perhaps more easily, think about things too little. As Socrates said, "The unexamined life is not worth living."

Finally, my entire adventure in Crete and Greece has involved something of a dance with <u>the arts</u>. At first I was drawn by the craft and beauty of the Minoans and the classical Greeks, as well as by the creative works of Kazantzakis. Then I became involved in teaching and sharing with various students the deeper aesthetic qualities inherent within these diverse forms of art. In the end, I myself began to get involved in creating objects of art out of the limestone and alabaster indigenous to Crete. Over the years I have sculpted quite a number of smaller pieces, to give to my friends as gifts, as well as several larger works in an effort to satisfy my own aesthetic drive and judgment. Although I have no plans, nor ability, to explore such artistic modes as poetry, painting, and music, I am still taking Cretan folkdancing lessons! To be sure, this present book hardly qualifies as a literary work of art. Nevertheless, I do hope it serves as an interesting and perhaps useful distillation of an extremely significant aspect of one person's romance with the island of Crete.